CW01647648

بسم الله الرحمن الرحيم

AN INTRODUCTION TO

Ṣaḥīḥ al-Bukhārī

AUTHOR'S BIOGRAPHY, RECENSIONS AND MANUSCRIPTS

AN INTRODUCTION TO

Ṣaḥīḥ al-Bukhārī

AUTHOR'S BIOGRAPHY, RECENSIONS AND MANUSCRIPTS

MUṢṬAFĀ AL-AʿẒAMĪ

Translation, Notes and Appendices

MUNTASIR ZAMAN

TURATH PUBLISHING

ISBN: 978-1-906949-51-8

Published by:
Turath Publishing
79 Mitcham Road London SW17 9PD
www.turath.co.uk +44 (20) 8767 3666

Author Muṣṭafā al-Aʿẓamī
Translation Muntasir Zaman
Editor Andrew Booso
General Editor Yahya Batha

British Library Cataloguing in Publication Data
Muṣṭafā al-Aʿẓamī
An Introduction to Ṣaḥīḥ al-Bukhārī
I. Title

Design & typesetting ARM (www.whitethreadpress.com)
Printed by Mega Printers, Istanbul

Distributors for UK and Europe
Azhar Academy Ltd.
54–56 Little Ilford Lane, London E12 5QA
trade@azharacademy.com
www.azharacademy.com

Distributors for South Africa
Darul-Ihsan Research and Education Centre
www.darulihsan.com

In memory of the scholar who produced

the first printed edition of *Ṣaḥīḥ al-Bukhārī*

Aḥmad ʿAlī as-Sahāranpūrī

(d. 1297 AH/1880 CE)

May his legacy never be forgotten

Yaḥyā ibn Jaʿfar al-Bīkandī (d. 243 AH) said,

"If I could increase the lifespan of Muḥammad ibn Ismāʿīl [al-Bukhārī] by sacrificing mine, I would have done so because my death would be the death of one man, but his death would result in the loss of knowledge."

(Baghdādī, *Tārīkh Baghdād*, 2:345)

Contents

Translator's Preface

It was a momentous occasion for Abū Ḥātim al-Harawī (d. 368 AH) when, after tireless effort and dedication, he had officially completed the reading of *Ṣaḥīḥ al-Bukhārī* to his teacher. As the recitation of the *Ṣaḥīḥ* concluded, he asked his teacher, "Did Firabrī himself recite every ḥadīth to you?" To Abū Ḥātim's dismay, the teacher replied, "No, rather we heard the ḥadīths being recited to him." Unaware of this, Abū Ḥātim up until this point had prefaced the reading of each ḥadīth with the words "Firabrī narrated to you." While such minutiae in the transmission process may have been trivial to many, for Abū Ḥātim it fell far short of the scholarly integrity requisite for narrating Prophetic ḥadīths. Thus, as a timeless gesture of fidelity and commitment, he recited the entire *Ṣaḥīḥ* to his teacher once more, only this time with the appropriate phrase of transmission.[1]

This meticulous approach to transmitting sacred knowledge is also displayed in the case of Saʿd ibn ʿAlī al-Qāḍī. In 475 AH, he claimed that he heard *Ṣaḥīḥ al-Bukhārī* via one link from Firabrī, who had passed away 120 years prior. This farfetched claim was enough of a reason for Saʿd's contemporaries to declare him a liar.[2]

Muslims rightfully pride themselves on preserving their sacred sources. This is evidenced by the countless volumes produced by scholars documenting the lives of thousands of ḥadīth narrators found in the chains of transmission (*isnād*). For example, a researcher can easily access the biographical accounts of all the narrators whom Imām Bukhārī (d. 256 AH) cites in his *Ṣaḥīḥ*. Not only that, scholars

1 Baghdādī, *Kifāyah*, 303–304.

2 Dhahabī, *Mīzān al-Iʿtidāl*, 2:124; Ibn Ḥajar, *Lisān al-Mīzān*, 4:32.

even preserved the biographical details of those who transmitted the *Ṣaḥīḥ* from its author in subsequent generations. Ibn Nuqṭah's (d. 629 AH) *at-Taqyīd li-Maʿrifat Ruwāt as-Sunan wa 'l-Masānīd*, for one, systematically documents the lives of those who transmitted these works. By extension, the authorship of Ḥadīth literature became definitively known to the point that Ibn aṣ-Ṣalāḥ (d. 643 AH) states that the major Ḥadīth books have circulated too widely to be tampered with or interpolated, let alone have their authorship doubted.[1] Whilst acknowledging this unparalleled scholarship, Aloys Sprenger (d. 1893) writes, "There is no nation nor has there been any like these [Muslims] which has, during twelve centuries, recorded the life of every man of letters."[2]

It can easily be said that no compilation of ḥadīth has garnered scholarly attention as Imām Abū ʿAbdillāh Muḥammad ibn Ismāʿīl al-Bukhārī's magnum opus, *al-Jāmiʿ al-Musnad aṣ-Ṣaḥīḥ al-Mukhtaṣar min Umūr Rasūlillāh wa Sunanihi wa Ayyāmihi*, commonly referred to as *Ṣaḥīḥ al-Bukhārī*.[3] This work was the result of sixteen years of relentless effort. With at least 400 scholarly works that expound on the text and 2000 extant manuscripts written in various periods of history to its name, there is hardly a book in human history that has received as much care and attention as *Ṣaḥīḥ al-Bukhārī*.[4]

One of the most thorough scholarly projects concerning *Ṣaḥīḥ al-Bukhārī* occurred around the year 666 AH, when a renowned Levantine Ḥadīth scholar, Sharaf ad-Dīn al-Yūnīnī (d. 701 AH), headed

---

1 Ibn aṣ-Ṣalāḥ, *Muqaddimah*, 17.

2 Sprenger, Foreword, in *A Biographical Dictionary of Persons Who Knew Mohammed*, 1:1. He then writes, "If the biographical records of the Musalmans were collected, we should probably have accounts of the lives of half a million of distinguished persons, and it would be found that there is not a decennium of their history, nor a place of importance which has not its representatives." Notwithstanding that half a million is an exaggeration, there is no doubt that Islamic civilization is peerless in this accomplishment. See Abū Ghuddah, *Lamaḥāt*, 163.

3 Bukhārī, as reflected in this text, is often referred to as Abū ʿAbdillāh or Muḥammad ibn Ismāʿīl.

4 Ḥusaynī, *Ithāf al-Qārī bi-Maʿrifat Juhūd wa Aʿmāl al-ʿUlamāʾ ʿalā Ṣaḥīḥ al-Bukhārī*, 6; *al-Fahras ash-Shāmil li 't-Turāth al-ʿArabī al-Islāmī al-Makhṭūṭ*, 493–565.

a legendary audition of *Ṣaḥīḥ al-Bukhārī* in Damascus. With the aid of the celebrated linguist Ibn Mālik (d. 672 AH), Yūnīnī convened a gathering of scholars who utilized a variety of critically-acclaimed manuscripts of the *Ṣaḥīḥ* for cross-reference in order to produce a meticulously authenticated version of the *Ṣaḥīḥ*. This was one of the most awe-inspiring episodes of literature-preservation in history. Subsequently, the historian and scribe Shihāb ad-Dīn an-Nuwayrī (d. 733 AH) transcribed several copies of what became known as the *Yūnīniyyah*, one of which is found in the Köprülü library in Istanbul.

The late Dr Muṣṭafā al-Aʿẓamī produced a facsimile edition of Nuwayrī's manuscript of *Ṣaḥīḥ al-Bukhārī* for the benefit of a wider readership. He prefaced the manuscript with an introduction in Arabic that serves as a useful starting point for anyone interested in advancing their knowledge of the *Ṣaḥīḥ* and its author. This introduction can be divided into three chapters. The first chapter explores Imām Bukhārī's biography and oeuvre. It then proceeds to important discussions on the modus operandi of his *Ṣaḥīḥ*, addressing key issues such as criteria of narrator-selection, stages of compilation and recensions. The first chapter concludes with an extensive list of transmitters and sub-transmitters of the *Ṣaḥīḥ*. The second chapter sheds light on the role of the *isnād* system in Islamic scholarship, with specific reference to the preservation of the Ḥadīth literature. Here the author cites his personal chain of transmission for *Ṣaḥīḥ al-Bukhārī* leading back to Imām Bukhārī. The third chapter delves into the *Yūnīniyyah* manuscript of *Ṣaḥīḥ al-Bukhārī*. The author provides biographical information on the manuscript's eponym, details secondary and tertiary copies, and reproduces the reading certificates and appended material on the manuscript.

The original Arabic introduction to Dr Aʿẓamī's edition was preceded by a partial English translation by his son Anas. However, there was a need to complete the translation, annotate relevant passages, and add appendices in order to refine the introduction. The present work hopes to accomplish this need. To make the work more reader-friendly, an idiomatic translation has been adopted and liberties have been taken in omitting and rearranging passages. The original footnotes and references have been retained, even if the edition used by Dr Aʿẓamī is unknown or the page references are not altogether clear. Notes were added to the relevant areas to provide clarity and supplemental material; these were placed in square brackets and marked with "Trans." I have added two appendices to make the work more comprehensive: the first establishes the reliability of the *Ṣaḥīḥ*'s primary transmitter, Muḥammad ibn Yūsuf al-Firabrī (d. 320 AH), and the second discusses an invaluable manuscript of the *Ṣaḥīḥ* that was transcribed by the Indian lexicographer Raḍī ad-Dīn aṣ-Ṣaghānī (d. 650 AH).

Translating and annotating this introduction has been a wonderful and edifying experience, but it was not without its challenges. I am indebted to many people who have made this process easier. My dear friend Maulana Haroon Anis has always been an invaluable resource for deciphering abstruse passages and providing relevant reading material. Andrew Booso was readily available to share editorial advice. I cannot put into words the immense support that I received from my beloved wife from the moment I began this project. Without her encouragement, patience and charismatic presence, this translation would have never seen the light of day. Despite her pregnancy, she affectionately catered to my needs and patiently bore with me as I spent countless hours typing away in translation and research. Thereafter, our baby daughter Husna proved to be an excellent assistant (in her own unique way) during the final phase of editing the translation. It goes without saying that my parents' sacrifices and prayers are the only reason I am able to do the little that I do. May Allah reward all of them with the best of this life and the Hereafter! All that is correct is from Allah, and all shortcomings are from me.

MUNTASIR ZAMAN
February 2019 | Dallas, Texas

Chapter 1

IMĀM BUKHĀRĪ'S LIFE AND TIMES

After an intermission in sending prophets, Allah ﷻ sent Muḥammad ﷺ and thereby sealed the institution of prophethood. He universalized his message for all of creation—including jinn and mankind, Arab and non-Arab—and made it unrestricted by the limits of time and place. Through His sheer mercy and kindness, Allah ﷻ has taken the responsibility of preserving His Book from all forms of adulteration, for He states, "We have sent down the Qur'ān Ourself, and We Ourself will guard it."[1] Furthermore, He directed towards it the hearts of His sincere believing slaves, the pious and righteous. Thus, they remain occupied with it during the hours of the night and throughout the day in memorization, teaching, correct pronunciation of its verses, ritual recitation, contemplation, study and practice.

Allah's direct promise to protect His Book entails an indirect promise to protect His Prophet's Sunna, because it elucidates and clarifies [the Book] as well as having legislative authority itself. Allah says, "We have sent down the message to you too [Prophet], so that you can explain to people what was sent for them, so that they may reflect."[2] While describing His Prophet, He says, "And who makes good things lawful to them and bad things unlawful."[3] Just as Allah enlisted His bondsmen to protect His Book, He also enlisted many

1 Sūrat al-Ḥijr, 9.
2 Sūrat an-Naḥl, 44.
3 Sūrat al-Aʿrāf, 157.

attentive, sincere, righteous and pure individuals—the likes of whom in their purity were never witnessed by the heavens—for the service of His Prophet's Sunna through study, practice, preservation and dissemination.

Hundreds of thousands of the greatest of this civilization have sacrificed their lives for the service of the Prophetic Sunna. Allah ﷻ created them for this purpose, so he endowed them with phenomenal memory, granted them sincerity, made the pen subservient to them, put time in their service, and conferred blessings in their lives and deeds. As a result, a voluminous and unparalleled library of Ḥadīth was produced. They diversified their methods in the field by utilizing every means at their disposal.[1] To proceed: it was in this academic atmosphere that Imām Bukhārī ؒ was born in a house of knowledge and piety.

Family

[His grandfather was] Ibrāhīm ibn al-Mughīrah ibn Bardizbah al-Juʿfī. Mughīrah embraced Islam at the hands of al-Yamān al-Juʿfī, who was the governor of Bukhara and the grandfather of the Ḥadīth scholar ʿAbdullāh ibn Muḥammad ibn Jaʿfar ibn Yamān al-Juʿfī al-Musnidī.[2]

In *Kitāb ath-Thiqāt*, Ibn Ḥibbān includes Ismāʿīl ibn Ibrāhīm, Bukhārī's father, and states, "He narrates from Ḥammād ibn Zayd and Mālik, and the Iraqis narrate from him."[3] In *at-Tārīkh al-Kabīr*, Bukhārī writes, "Ismāʿīl ibn Ibrāhīm ibn al-Mughīrah heard from Mālik and Ḥammād ibn Zayd, and he accompanied Ibn al-Mubārak." In *Tārīkh al-Islām*, Dhahabī writes, "Bukhārī's father was among the scrupulous scholars. He narrated from Abū Muʿāwiyah and others. Aḥmad ibn

1 On the diverse styles of authorship adopted by the Ḥadīth scholars, see Kattānī's *ar-Risālah al-Mustaṭrafah fī Bayān Mashhūr Kutub as-Sunnah al-Musharrafah*.

2 [Ismāʿīl al-ʿAjlūnī (d. 1162 AH) writes that he did not come across any mention of Imām Bukhārī getting married, let alone having any children. See ʿAjlūnī, *Iḍāʾat al-Badrayn*, 3. On the other hand, Bakr ibn Munīr relates an incident involving Bukhārī and "his son Aḥmad." See Baghdādī, *Tārīkh Baghdād*, 6:156; Dhahabī, *Siyar Aʿlām an-Nubalāʾ*, 12:447. However, al-Ḥākim clearly states that Bukhārī and Muslim left behind no male offspring. See al-Ḥākim, *Maʿrifat ʿUlūm al-Ḥadīth*, 51. Trans.]

3 *Thiqāt*, 8:98.

Jaʿfar and Naṣr ibn al-Ḥusayn narrated from him."[1] Isḥāq ibn Aḥmad ibn Khalaf said that he heard Bukhārī say, "My father heard from Mālik ibn Anas, saw Ḥammād ibn Zayd, and shook hands with Ibn al-Mubārak using both hands."[2] Aḥmad ibn Ḥafṣ states, "I came to Abū 'l-Ḥusayn Ismāʿīl ibn Ibrāhīm during his final moments and he said, 'I do not know of a single dirham from all my assets that was earned through dubious means.'"

It was into this family of piety and knowledge that Imām Bukhārī was born on the 13 Shawwāl 194 AH after the Jumuʿah prayer in Bukhara. Muḥammad ibn Aḥmad al-Balkhī relates from his father that Muḥammad ibn Ismāʿīl lost his sight during his childhood. His mother then had a dream of Ibrāhīm ﷺ who gave her glad tidings, "Indeed, Allah has restored your son's sight."[3] He lost his father at a young age and was reared by his righteous mother. Allah blessed him with a miraculous memory, just as He inspired him to be particular with his time. Bukhārī began writing at an early age. By age of eighteen, he authored *Qaḍāyā aṣ-Ṣaḥābah wa 't-Tābiʿīn* (Verdicts of the Companions and the Successors). There are countless works, lengthy and brief, to his name.

Travels, Study and Authorship

Muḥammad ibn Abī Ḥātim al-Warrāq, Bukhārī's copyist, states,

> I asked Abū ʿAbdillāh Muḥammad ibn Ismāʿīl al-Bukhārī, "How did you begin your study of Ḥadīth?" He replied, "I was inspired to memorize ḥadīths while I was still in school."
>
> *Correcting his teacher*: I then asked, "How old were you?" He said, "I

1 *Tārīkh al-Islām*, 19:239.

2 *Siyar Aʿlām an-Nubalāʾ*, 12:393; *Ṭabaqāt ash-Shāfiʿiyyah al-Kubrā*, 2:213.

3 *Siyar Aʿlām an-Nubalāʾ*, 12:393; *Hudā as-Sārī*, 478. [*Hudā as-Sārī* is Ḥāfiẓ Ibn Ḥajar al-ʿAsqalānī's prolegomenon to *Fatḥ al-Bārī*, his commentary on *Ṣaḥīḥ al-Bukhārī*. The title of the prolegomenon is commonly vowelized as *Hady as-Sārī*, but the correct vowelization is *Hudā as-Sārī*. This is based on Ibn Ḥajar's handwritten vowelization of the title in one of the manuscripts of the book. Moreover, the word *hudā* is linguistically more appropriate than *hady* in this context. See the editor's preface to the ar-Risālah al-ʿĀlamiyyah edition of *Fatḥ al-Bārī* (2013) 1:38; ʿAwwāmah, annotations on *al-Madkhal ilā ʿIlm as-Sunan*, 2:615. Trans.]

was ten years old or younger. I left school when I was ten. I frequented the study-circle of Dākhilī and others. One day while teaching, Dākhilī said, 'Sufyān, from Abū 'z-Zubayr, from Ibrāhīm.' I told him, 'Abū 'z-Zubayr did not narrate from Ibrāhīm,' but he rebuked me. I said to him, 'Consult your source-text.' He went home, consulted the source-text, returned, and said, 'How is it supposed to be?' I said, 'It is Zubayr ibn ʿAdī, from Ibrāhīm.' He took my pen, amended his book, and said, 'You were right.'"

Bukhārī was asked, "How old were you when you corrected him?" He said, "Eleven years old. At the age of sixteen, I memorized the works of Ibn al-Mubārak and Wakīʿ, and I was versed in the discourse of these people [i.e. the partisans of *ra'y*]. I then left with my mother and brother Aḥmad to Makkah. After completing the pilgrimage, my brother returned with my mother while I remained behind in the pursuit of Ḥadīth."[1]

He also said,

Authoring Books: I heard Abū ʿAbdillāh Muḥammad ibn Ismāʿīl say, "At the age of eighteen, I began compiling the verdicts and verbal proclamations of the Companions and the Successors. This was during the era of ʿUbaydullāh ibn Mūsā. At that time, I wrote the *Tārīkh* by the Prophet's grave during the moonlit nights. Nearly everyone in history has an anecdote [that I could document], but I disliked lengthening the book."[2]

Academic Adjudication: And I heard him say, "I came to Ḥumaydī once when I was eighteen years old. He was disputing an issue related to Ḥadīth with someone. When Ḥumaydī saw me, he proclaimed, 'The one to adjudicate between us has arrived.' When they both presented their arguments to me, I judged in Ḥumaydī's favour. His interlocutor would have died a disbeliever had he persisted and died upon his claim."[3]

1 *Tārīkh Baghdād*, 2:7; *Siyar Aʿlām an-Nubalā'*, 12:393.

2 *Siyar Aʿlām an-Nubalā'*, 12:400.

3 Ibid., 12:401.

Al-Faḍl ibn Isḥāq al-Bazzāz said: Aḥmad ibn Minhāl al-ʿĀbid narrated to us that Abū Bakr al-Aʿyan said, "We wrote from Bukhārī at the door of Muḥammad ibn Yūsuf al-Firyābī and he did not have facial hair. We asked, 'How old are you?' He said, 'Seventeen years old.'"[1]

Isḥāq ibn Rāhawayh told his students, "You should compile an abridgment on the Prophet's *sunan*." This remark settled in Bukhārī's heart. Abū ʿAbdillāh [al-Bukhārī] said, "I was in the company of Isḥāq ibn Rāhawayh when one of our companions said, 'You should compile an abridgement of the Prophet's *sunan*. That settled in my heart, so I set out to compile this book.'"[2]

Muḥammad ibn Abī Ḥātim said,

> I heard Bukhārī say, "I entered Baghdad for the eighth and final time—each time I sat with Aḥmad ibn Ḥanbal. As I bade him farewell, he said, 'Abū ʿAbdillāh, how could you leave knowledge and the scholars, and return to Khurasan?' I still recall his words to this day."[3]

Abū ʿAbd [Allāh] al-Ḥākim writes that Bukhārī first arrived in Nishapur in 209 AH and visited again for the final time in 250 AH, whereupon he resided and taught Ḥadīth for five years consecutively.

[Muḥammad ibn Yūsuf al-Firabrī] said, "While staying in Bukhārī's house one night, I observed that he rose and lit the lamp at least eighteen times to make notes of things that came to his mind." Muḥammad ibn Abī Ḥātim said, "During our travels, Abū ʿAbdillāh and I would share a house except during the midsummer days. He would rise fifteen to twenty times in one night, lighting a lamp each time to write ḥadīths and take notes."[4]

---

1 Ibid.

2 Ibid. [A number of factors motivated Imām Bukhārī to compile his *Ṣaḥīḥ*. Apart from Ibn Rāhawayh's suggestion mentioned here, the main factor was a desire to gather rigorously authentic Prophetic ḥadīths. A third factor was a dream that Bukhārī had involving the Prophet ﷺ, which was interpreted as him being chosen to dispel lies against the Prophet ﷺ. See Ibn Ḥajar, *Hudā as-Sārī*, 6–7. In *al-Wajh aṣ-Ṣabīḥ fī Khatm al-Jamiʿ aṣ-Ṣaḥīḥ*, Ibn ʿAllān (d. 1057 AH) opines that all three factors collectively motivated him. See ʿAwwāmah, annotations on *Tadrīb ar-Rāwī*, 2:266. Trans.]

3 Ibid., 12:403.

4 Ibid., 12:404.

Hāni' ibn an-Naḍr said,

> We were in the company of Muḥammad ibn Yūsuf al-Firyābī in the Levant. We enjoyed ourselves like young men eating mulberries and the like. Muḥammad ibn Ismāʿīl was with us, but he did not partake in our activities; he was busy seeking knowledge.[1]

Imām Bukhārī details his dedication to seeking knowledge in the following words:

> During my stay in Nishapur, I would receive letters from my relatives in Bukhara conveying their greetings. I would intend to respond to their greetings, but their names would escape me, so I never replied—however, rarely did I forget knowledge.

Explaining his method of writing as a student, he said,

> My writing of ḥadīth was unlike that of others: If I wrote from a competent narrator, I asked him his name, agnomen, affiliation and background in Ḥadīth. Yet if he was lacking [such competency], I requested his source-text and copied it. As for others, they care little about what they write or how they write it.[2]

Memory, Knowledge and Intelligence

In *Tārīkh Bukhārā*, Muḥammad ibn Aḥmad Ghunjār said,

> I heard Abū 'Amr Aḥmad ibn Muḥammad al-Muqri': I heard Mahīb ibn Sulaym: I heard Jaʿfar ibn Muḥammad ibn al-Qaṭṭān, the Imām of Karmīniyah: I heard Muḥammad ibn Ismāʿīl say, "I wrote from over a thousand teachers, and from each teacher over ten thousand ḥadīths. I remember the chain for every ḥadīth that I know."[3]

Muḥammad ibn Abī Ḥātim said,

1 Ibid., 12:405.

2 Ibid., 12:406. The editor vowelized the word *wa nasakhtuhu* ("and I copied it") incorrectly as *wa nuskhatuhu* ("and his copy"), leading others to do the same.

3 Ibid., 12:407.

> Abū ʿAbdillāh read to us *Kitāb al-Hibah* (the Book of Gifting) and said, "Wakīʿ's treatise on gifting only contains two or three *musnad* ḥadīths [i.e. via unbroken chains] and ʿAbdullāh ibn al-Mubārak's collections contain roughly five. However, this book of mine contains five hundred or more."
>
> I heard Abū ʿAbdillāh say, "I thought about the students of Anas and three-hundred names came to mind immediately." I also heard him say, "I never visited anyone except that they benefited from me more than I benefited from them."[1]

Aḥyad ibn Abī Jaʿfar, the governor of Bukhara, said,

> Muḥammad ibn Ismāʿīl once said, "At times, I would write in the Levant a ḥadīth that I heard in Basra, and I would write in Egypt a ḥadīth that I heard in the Levant." I asked, "Abū ʿAbdillāh, in its entirety?" He remained silent.[2]

Bukhārī once said, "I did not sleep last night until I counted the number of ḥadīths included in my works: there were roughly two-hundred thousand *musnad* ḥadīths."[3] Abū Bakr al-Kalwādhānī said, "I never saw anyone like Muḥammad ibn Ismāʿīl: he would borrow a book from scholars, examine it briefly, and memorize most of the *aṭrāf* (first parts) of its ḥadīths."

Muḥammad ibn Yūsuf al-Firabrī said,

> I heard Abū Jaʿfar Muḥammad ibn Abī Ḥātim al-Warrāq say in the appendix to Abū ʿAbdillāh's *Shamāʾil*—I [Dhahabī] say: this is not found in the recension of Ibn Khalaf ash-Shīrāzī—"I heard Muḥammad ibn Ismāʿīl al-Bukhārī say, 'I did not start teaching ḥadīth until I recognized authentic from dubious, studied the books of *raʾy*, and visited Basra nearly five times. While there [in Basra], I wrote down every authentic ḥadīth found in Basra, except for what did not become apparent to me.'"[4]

1 Ibid., 12:411.

2 Ibid.

3 Ibid., 12:412.

4 Ibid., 12:416.

Yaḥyā ibn Jaʿfar al-Bīkandī said, "If I could increase Muḥammad ibn Ismāʿīl's lifespan by sacrificing mine, I would have done so because my death would be the death of one man, but his death would result in the loss of knowledge." He once told Bukhārī, "Were it not for you, I would find no pleasure in living in Bukhara."[1]

Scholarly Praise

Nuʿaym ibn Ḥammād said, "Muḥammad ibn Ismāʿīl is the jurist of this Community (*ummah*)."[2] Yaʿqūb ibn Ibrāhīm ad-Dawraqī said, "Muḥammad ibn Ismāʿīl is the jurist of this Community."[3]

Muḥammad ibn Abī Ḥātim said,

> I heard Abū ʿAbdillāh say, "The students of ʿAmr ibn ʿAlī al-Fallās discussed a particular ḥadīth with me, and I said, 'I do not recognize it.' They were pleased to know that, so they informed ʿAmr, who said, 'A ḥadīth not recognized by Muḥammad ibn Ismāʿīl is not a ḥadīth.'"[4]

Muḥammad ibn Yūsuf said,

> We were with Abū ʿAbdillāh in the company of Muḥammad ibn Bashshār, who asked him about a ḥadīth and he responded. He then said, "This is the most knowledgeable of Allah's creation in our times," pointing to Muḥammad ibn Ismāʿīl.[5]

Ismāʿīl ibn Abī Uways said,

> No one has taken [ḥadīths] from me like Muḥammad [ibn Ismāʿīl]: he noticed that my source-texts were worn out, so he said, "Would you permit me to re-write them for you?" I responded affirmatively. He extracted all my ḥadīths with this ruse.[6]

Muḥammad ibn Yaʿqūb, the Ḥadīth expert, relates from his father, "I

1 Ibid., 12:418.
2 Ibid., 12:419.
3 Ibid., 12:424.
4 Ibid., 12:420.
5 Ibid., 12:429.
6 Ibid., 12:430.

saw Muslim ibn al-Ḥajjāj sit in front of Bukhārī, asking him questions [by humbling himself] like a child."[1] Muḥammad ibn Ḥamdūn said, "I heard Muslim ibn al-Ḥajjāj tell Bukhārī, 'O teacher of teachers, master of the Ḥadīth scholars, expert of subtle defects in ḥadīths, allow me to kiss your feet.'"

Abū ʿĪsā at-Tirmidhī said, "I have not seen anyone in Iraq or Khurasan more knowledgeable than Muḥammad ibn Ismāʿīl vis-à-vis subtle defects [in ḥadīths], history, and familiarity with chains of transmission."[2]

Dhahabī relates an interesting anecdote from Abū 'l-Khaṭṭāb ibn Diḥyah:

> Ramlī the Liar said, "Bukhārī is unknown: no one besides Firabrī transmitted from him." In response, Abū 'l-Khaṭṭāb said,
>
> By Allah, he has lied in this matter and transgressed. May his mouth be filled with rocks! Bukhārī is celebrated for knowledge and its acquisition; his memory and brilliance are undisputed; he travelled far and wide, seeking out reports and chains of transmission. Many scholars have narrated from him. As for his compilation, he presented it to the Ḥadīth expert of his age, Abū Zurʿah, who said, "Your book is authentic apart from three narrations."[3]

Teachers and Students

Before he travelled abroad, he studied Ḥadīth in Bukhara with ʿAbdullāh ibn Muḥammad ibn ʿAbdillāh ibn Jaʿfar ibn al-Yamān

1 Ibid., 12:432.

2 Ibid., 12:432.

3 Ibid., 12:438. [A marginal note in the manuscript of *Siyar* states that the last part of this report is an oversight from Ibn Diḥyah, because it was Imām Muslim, not Imam Bukhārī, who presented his *Ṣaḥīḥ* to Abū Zurʿah. See the editor's annotation on *Siyar*, op. cit. It is reported, however, that Bukhārī presented the *Ṣaḥīḥ* to a number of experts including Aḥmad ibn Ḥanbal, Yaḥyā ibn Maʿīn and ʿAlī ibn al-Madīnī. See Ibn Khayr, *Fihrist*, 132. Although there are some issues with this report's chain of transmission, given that the aforementioned experts were Bukhārī's direct teachers, it is not difficult to accept that he could have presented the *Ṣaḥīḥ* to them. See Khaldūn al-Aḥdab, *al-Imām al-Bukhārī wa Jāmiʿuhu aṣ-Ṣaḥīḥ*, p. 116; Brown, *The Canonization of al-Bukhārī and Muslim*, 94 (note 163). Trans.]

al-Juʿfī al-Musnidī, Muḥammad ibn Salām al-Bīkandī and others who were not his senior teachers. In Balkh, he heard from Makkī ibn Ibrāhīm, one of his senior teachers. In Merv, he heard from ʿAbdān ibn ʿUthmān, ʿAlī ibn al-Ḥasan ibn Shaqīq, Ṣadaqah ibn al-Faḍl and others. In Nishapur, [he heard] from Yaḥyā ibn Yaḥyā and others. In Rayy, he heard from Ibrāhīm ibn Mūsā. In Baghdad, when he travelled to Iraq in the latter part of 210 AH, he heard from Muḥammad ibn ʿĪsā aṭ-Ṭabbāʿ, Surayj ibn an-Nuʿmān, Muḥammad ibn Sābiq and ʿAffān. In Basra, [he heard] from Abū ʿĀṣim an-Nabīl, Anṣārī, ʿAbd ar-Raḥmān ibn Ḥammād ash-Shuʿaythī—the student of Ibn ʿAwn, Muḥammad ibn ʿArʿarah, Ḥajjāj ibn Minhāl, Badal ibn al-Muḥabbar, ʿAbdullāh ibn Rajāʾ, and many others. In Kufa, he heard from ʿUbaydullāh ibn Mūsā, Abū Nuʿaym, Khalid ibn Makhlad, Ṭalq ibn Ghannām, Khālid ibn Yazīd al-Muqriʾ (with whom he studied the Qurʾānic recital according to Ḥamzah). In Makkah, he heard from Abū ʿAbd ar-Raḥmān al-Muqriʾ, Khallād ibn Yaḥyā, Ḥassān ibn Ḥassān al-Baṣrī, Abū ʾl-Walīd Aḥmad ibn Muḥammad al-Azraqī and Ḥumaydī. In Madīnah, he heard from ʿAbd al-ʿAzīz al-Uwaysī, Ayyūb ibn Sulaymān ibn Bilāl and Ismāʿīl ibn Abī Uways. In Egypt, he heard from Saʿīd ibn Abī Maryam, Aḥmad ibn Ishkāb, ʿAbdullāh ibn Yūsuf, Aṣbagh, and many others. In the Levant, he heard from Abū ʾl-Yamān, Ādam ibn Abī Iyās, ʿAlī ibn ʿAyyāsh and Bishr ibn Shuʿayb. In addition, he heard from Abū ʾl-Mughīrah ʿAbd al-Quddūs, Aḥmad ibn Khālid al-Wahbī, Muḥammad ibn Yusuf al-Firyābī, Abū Mushir, and many others.

Muḥammad ibn Abī Ḥātim said,

> I heard him saying, "When I arrived in Balkh, the locals asked me to dictate to them from every teacher I wrote ḥadīths from. So, I dictated a thousand ḥadīths from a thousand teachers I had written from." A month before his demise, I heard him say, "I wrote from 1,080 people, each a partisan of Ḥadīth who opined that faith (īmān) is a verbal proclamation and action; it increases and decreases."[1]

---

1 Ibid., 12:395.

Bukhārī narrated from Muḥammad ibn Yaḥyā adh-Dhuhlī abundantly—but concealed his name (*yudallisuhu*), Muḥammad ibn ʿAbdillāh al-Mukharrimī and Muḥammad ibn ʿAbd ar-Raḥīm Ṣāʿiqah—they were his peers.

He heard from Abū Mushir, but he was uncertain whether he heard directly. He mentions outside of the *Ṣaḥīḥ*, "Abū Mushir narrated to us, or someone narrated to us from him."

He narrated from Aḥmad ibn ʿAbd al-Malik ibn Wāqid al-Ḥarrānī, whom he met in Iraq.

He never entered Algeria. He said, "I visited Muʿallā ibn Manṣūr ar-Rāzī in Baghdad in the year [2]10 AH."

Countless people narrated from him, among whom were Abū ʿĪsā at-Tirmidhī, Abū Ḥātim, Ibrāhīm ibn Isḥāq al-Ḥarbī, Abū Bakr ibn Abī 'd-Dunyā, Abū Bakr Aḥmad ibn ʿAmr ibn Abī ʿĀṣim, Ṣāliḥ ibn Muḥammad Jazarah, Muḥammad ibn ʿAbdillāh al-Ḥaḍramī Muṭayyan, Ibrāhīm ibn Maʿqil an-Nasafī, ʿAbdullāh ibn Nājiyah, Abū Bakr Muḥammad ibn Isḥāq ibn Khuzaymah, ʿUmar ibn Muḥammad ibn Bujayr, Abū Quraysh Muḥammad ibn Jumuʿah, Yaḥyā ibn Muḥammad ibn Ṣāʿid, Muḥammad ibn Yūsuf—the transmitter of the *Ṣaḥīḥ*, Manṣūr ibn Muḥammad Mizbazdah [*sic*], Abū Bakr ibn Abī Dāwūd, Ḥusayn and Qāsim the sons of Maḥāmilī, ʿAbdullāh ibn Muḥammad ibn al-Ashqar, Muḥammad ibn Sulaymān ibn Fāris, Maḥmūd ibn ʿAnbar an-Nasafī, and countless others. Muslim also narrated from him outside his *Ṣaḥīḥ*. It is said that Nasaʾī narrated from him in the chapter of fasting in his *Sunan*, but this is not accurate. However, in his *Kunā*, Nasaʾī relates material via ʿAbdullāh ibn Aḥmad al-Khaffāf from Bukhārī.[1]

Demise

After extensive travels in the pursuit of knowledge, he returned to his hometown Bukhara as a teacher where he was greeted by nearly the entire town. He stayed there for a few days until a conflict arose

1 Ibid., 12:396–397.

between him and Khālid ibn Aḥmad adh-Dhuhlī, the governor of Bukhara, so he was eventually ordered to leave the city.[1] It is said that the governor of Bukhara sent a message to Muḥammad ibn Ismāʿīl, "Bring me the *Jāmiʿ*, the *Tārīkh* and other books, so that I may hear them from you." Muḥammad ibn Ismāʿīl told the messenger,

> I will not humiliate knowledge by taking it to the doors of people. If you are interested, come to my house or the local masjid. If this does not please you, then you may prevent me from holding a study-circle—you are the sultan, after all—so that I have an excuse in the court of Allah, because I will not hoard knowledge due to the words of the Prophet, "Whoever is sought for knowledge but hides it, he will be bridled with reins of fire."

This was the cause of their conflict.[2] Thus, Muḥammad ibn Ismāʿīl left to Khartank where he stayed with family members.[3] One night, he was heard supplicating after the ʿIshāʾ prayer, "O Allah, the earth has become restricted for me despite its vastness, so take me back to You." He passed away before the end of the month. His grave is in Khartank.[4] He passed away on Friday on the eve of ʿĪd al-Fiṭr at the time of the ʿIshāʾ prayer. He was buried on Saturday after the Ẓuhr prayer on 1 Shawwāl 256 AH. He lived 13 days short of 82 years.

---

1 Ibid., 12:463.

2 [For more context on the roots of their conflict, see Dhahabī, *Siyar Aʿlām an-Nubalāʾ*, 12:617. Trans.]

3 [Ibn Ḥajar al-Haytamī relates that the locals of Khartank, a city near Samarqand, state that the area received its name after Imām Bukhārī's demise: Khartank means "crowded space," due to the crowds of people who visit Bukhārī's grave. See Haytamī, *Fatḥ al-Ilāh fī Sharḥ al-Mishkāh*, 1:79. It is worth noting, however, that Samʿānī mentions that Bukhārī passed away in the home of Abū Manṣūr Ghālib ibn Ibrāhīm, whose affiliation was Khartankī. See Samʿānī, *Ansāb*, 5:79. Trans.]

4 *Tārīkh Baghdād*, 2:34.

Works[1]

1. *Akhbār aṣ-Ṣifāt* (Reports on the Divine Attributes).[2]
2. *Al-Adab al-Mufrad* (The Independent Book on Manners). It was transmitted from Bukhārī by Aḥmad ibn Muḥammad ibn al-Jalīl al-Bazzār.[3] It has been published multiple times in various places.
3. *Asāmī aṣ-Ṣaḥābah* (Names of the Companions).[4] Ibn Mandah mentioned it.
4. *Kitāb Aṣḥāb an-Nabī* (Book on the Prophet's Companions).[5]
5. *Ashribah* (Drinks). Dāraquṭnī mentioned it in *al-Mu'talif wa 'l-Mukhtalif*.
6. *Iʿtiṣām* (The Adherence).[6]
7. *Kitāb al-Īmān* (Book of Faith).[7]
8. *Bad' al-Makhlūqāt* (Beginning of Creation).
9. *Birr al-Wālidayn* (Respect for Parents). Ustādh Niẓām Yaʿqūbī informed me that this book was discovered recently in Morocco and is currently being edited.[8]
10. *At-Tārīkh al-Awsaṭ* (The Medium History). There has been confusion between *at-Tārīkh al-Awsaṭ* and *at-Tārīkh aṣ-Ṣaghīr*. *At-Tārīkh al-Awsaṭ* was transmitted by Zanjawayh and Khaffāf, as

1 [A number of books may be added to this list, such as 1) *ar-Radd ʿalā 'l-Jahmiyyah*; 2) *Mashyakhah*; and 3) *Intiqā' al-Bukhārī min Ḥadīthihīi li-Ahl Baghdād*. To date, only about ten of the books listed here are published. There is little information about the nature of the other works. ʿAbd al-ʿAlīm al-Bastawī questions the ascription of some of these books to Imām Bukhārī, particularly *at-Tārīkh fī Maʿrifat Ruwāt al-Ḥadīth*, *at-Tawārīkh wa 'l-Ansāb*, *ʿAqīdah* and *Akhbār aṣ-Ṣifāt*. It is possible, he postulates, that these works were extracted from his other larger works; hence, they were not independent books compiled by Bukhārī. The same can be said about some of the other works listed here for which we have little to no information. See Mubārakfūrī, *Sīrat al-Imām al-Bukhārī*, 1:309–311. Trans.]

2 *Tārīkh at-Turāth al-ʿArabī*, 1:259.

3 *Hudā as-Sārī*, 492.

4 Ibid.

5 *At-Tārīkh al-Kabīr*, 1:2:60.

6 *Ṣaḥīḥ al-Bukhārī*, *Kitāb al-Iʿtiṣām*, no. 7271.

7 *At-Tārīkh al-Kabīr*, 1:2:158.

8 [*Birr al-Wālidayn* has recently been published several times. Trans.]

mentioned by Ibn Khayr in his *Fihrist.*[1] *At-Tārīkh aṣ-Ṣaghīr* was transmitted by ʿAbdullāh al-Ashqar.

11. *At-Tawārīkh wa 'l-Ansāb* (Chronologies and Genealogies). Fuat Sezgin mentioned it.[2]
12. *At-Tārīkh aṣ-Ṣaghīr* (The Minor History). This was transmitted from Bukhārī by ʿAbdullāh ibn Muḥammad al-Ashqar.[3] It is mentioned that several manuscripts of this work are available in Vancouver, Rampur, and Buhar Library in Calcutta, India. It is difficult to say with certainty that these are manuscripts of *at-Tārīkh aṣ-Ṣaghīr* owing to the confusion between *at-Tārīkh aṣ-Ṣaghīr* and *al-Awsaṭ*.
13. *At-Tārīkh fī Maʿrifat Ruwāt wa Naqalat al-Akhbār wa 's-Sunan wa Tamyīz Thiqātihim min Ḍuʿafāʾihim wa Tārīkh Wafātihim* (History: Recognizing the Narrators and Transmitters of Reports and *Sunan*, Distinguishing the Reliable Among them from the Weak, and the Chronologies of their Death Dates).[4]
14. *At-Tārīkh al-Kabīr* (The Major History). It was printed in Hyderabad, India.
15. *Kitāb at-Tafsīr al-Kabīr* (The Major Exegesis). Bukhārī's copyist said, "While in Firabr, I saw him lie down while authoring *Kitāb at-Tafsīr.*[5]
16. *Al-Jāmiʿ aṣ-Ṣaḥīḥ al-Mukhtaṣar al-Musnad min Umūr Rasūlillāh—ṣallallāhu ʿalayhi wa sallam—wa Sunanihi wa Ayyāmihi* (The Authentic Abridged *Musnad* Compendium of the Prophet's Affairs, Deeds and Days). Ibn Ḥajar said, "Ibrāhim ibn Maʿqil is among the transmitters of the *Jāmiʿ* whose recension reached us continuously through authorization. He missed a portion from the ending of the book, which he transmitted through authorization. Another transmitter is Ḥammād ibn Shākir an-Nasawī. The re-

1 *Hudā as-Sārī*, 492.
2 *Tārīkh at-Turāth*, 1:258.
3 *Hudā as-Sārī*, 492.
4 *Tārīkh at-Turāth*, 1:257.
5 *At-Tārīkh al-Kabīr*, 4:2:232 and 265; *Tārīkh Baghdād*, 2:14; *Hudā as-Sārī*, 492.

cension which has been transmitted through continuous audition in this era and before is that of Muḥammad ibn Yūsuf ibn Maṭar ibn Ṣāliḥ ibn Bishr al-Firabrī."[1]

17. *Al-Jāmiʿ aṣ-Ṣaghīr* (The Minor Compendium).[2]
18. *Al-Jāmiʿ al-Kabīr* (The Major Compendium). This book is lost. Ibn Ḥajar writes that Ibn Ṭāhir mentioned it.[3]
19. *Khalq Afʿāl al-ʿIbād* (Creating the Actions of the Bondsmen). This was transmitted from Bukhārī by both Yusuf ibn Rayḥān ibn ʿAbd aṣ-Ṣamad and Firabrī. It was printed several times.
20. *Rafʿ al-Yadayn fī 'ṣ-Ṣalāh* (Raising the Hands in Prayer). This was transmitted from Bukhārī by Maḥmūd ibn Isḥāq al-Khuzāʿī.
21. *Riqāq* (Softening the Hearts). Ḥājjī Khalīfah mentioned it.[4]
22. *As-Sunan fī 'l-Fiqh* (*Sunnah*s Related to Jurisprudence). Ibn Nadīm mentioned it in the *Fihrist*.[5]
23. *Aḍ-Ḍuʿafāʾ aṣ-Ṣaghīr* (The Minor Book on Weak Transmitters). This was transmitted from Bukhārī by Dawlābī, Abū Jaʿfar Musabbiḥ ibn Saʿīd and Ādam ibn Mūsā.[6]
24. *Aḍ-Ḍuʿafāʾ al-Kabīr* (The Major Book on Weak Transmitters).[7]
25. *Kitāb al-ʿAtīq* (The Ancient Book). In *at-Tarīkh al-Kabīr*, Bukhārī writes, "Bakr ibn Mubashshir: he narrated from Abū Yaḥyā, and Muḥammad ibn Yaḥyā narrated from him. He is Ḥijāzī, as found in *Kitāb al-ʿAtīq*."[8] He writes, "Thābit ibn Maʿbad al-Muḥāribī: Misʿar related his statement from ʿAyyāsh al-Kulaybī. In *ʿAtīq* there is no qualification."[9] He writes, "Sulaymān ibn Abī Sulaymān, the freed slave of Ibn ʿAbbās—as mentioned in *ʿAtīq*." He writes, "Jābir ibn Rustum al-Baṣrī: he narrated from Shaybah

---

1 *Hudā as-Sārī*, 492.
2 *Kashf aẓ-Ẓunūn*, 1:564.
3 *Hudā as-Sārī*, 492.
4 *Kashf aẓ-Ẓunūn*, 2:1420.
5 *Fihrist*, 322.
6 *Hudā as-Sārī*, 492.
7 [See, Bastawī, annotations on *Sīrat al-Imām al-Bukhārī*, 291–293. Trans.]
8 *At-Tārīkh al-Kabīr*, 1:2:95.
9 Ibid., 1:2:169.

ibn Niṣāḥ, and Zayd ibn Ḥubāb narrated from him—as found in *ʿAtīq*."[1]

26. *ʿAqīdah* (The Creed).
27. *Kitāb al-ʿIlal* (Hidden Defects). Ibn Mandah mentioned it.[2]
28. *Fawāʾid* (Useful Points). Tirmidhī mentioned this in his *Jāmiʿ* under the chapter of the Virtues of Abū Muḥammad Ṭalḥah ibn ʿUbaydillāh.[3]
29. *Al-Qirāʾah Khalf al-Imām* (Recitation behind the Imām). This was transmitted from Bukhārī by Maḥmūd ibn Isḥāq al-Khuzāʿī. There are several prints of this book.
30. *Qaḍāyā aṣ-Ṣaḥābah wa ʾt-Tābiʿīn wa Aqāwīlihim* (Verdicts and Pronouncements of the Companions and the Successors). This was his first book, which he wrote at the age of eighteen.[4]
31. *Kunā* (Agnomens). It was published in Hyderabad in 1360 AH/1941 CE.
32. *Mukhtaṣar* (The Abridgement).[5] In the entry of ʿUrs ibn ʿAmīrah in *at-Tārīkh al-Kabīr*, Bukhārī writes, "He is from the Companions. He said, 'I heard the Prophet say, "Indeed, a slave of Allah does the deeds of those destined for Paradise. . ."' I have explained this in *Kitāb al-Mukhtaṣar*."
33. *Kitāb al-Mabsūṭ* (The Extensive Compendium). Mahīb ibn Sulaym narrated it from Bukhārī.[6] Ḥāfiẓ Ibn Ḥajar said, "Khalīlī mentioned it in *Irshād*." See Mahīb ibn Sulaym's entry.[7]

1 Ibid., 1:2:204. [There appears to be no separate book entitled *ʿAtīq*. Rather, the references to *ʿAtīq* (lit. ancient) are from the transmitter of *at-Tārikh al-Kabīr* or Bukhārī himself whereby the given passage is found differently in an earlier edition of *at-Tārīkh al-Kabīr*. Hence, *Kitāb al-ʿAtīq*, *al-Kitāb al-ʿAtīq* and *ʿAtīq* are simply references to an earlier edition of the book. As will be mentioned later, Bukhārī revised *at-Tārīkh al-Kabīr* at least three times, so there are at minimum three editions of the book. See Muʿallimī's annotations—signed with the letter *ḥāʾ*— in *at-Tārīkh al-Kabīr*, 2:169, no. 89; cf. idem, "Introduction," in, *Muwaḍḍiḥ Awhām al-Jamʿ wa ʾt-Tafrīq*, 1:11–12. Trans.]

2 *Hudā as-Sārī*, 492.

3 *Jāmiʿ at-Tirmidhī*, 5:309.

4 *Tārīkh Baghdād*, 7:2.

5 *At-Tārīkh al-Kabīr*, 4:1:87.

6 *Hudā as-Sārī*, 492.

7 *Irshād*, 3:973.

34. *Al-Musnad [al-Kabīr]* (The Major Musnad). Firabrī mentioned it,[1] and Bukhārī said, "ʿAbdullāh ibn Abī Bakr aṣ-Ṣiddīq ibn Abī Quḥāfah: he is ʿAbdullāh ibn ʿAbdillāh ibn ʿUthmān at-Taymī al-Qurashī. He passed away before ʿUmar. He would frequent the Prophet while he was in the cave. We have explained this in the *Musnad*."[2]
35. *Kitāb al-Hibah* (The Book of Gifting), which comprises 500 ḥadīths or more. His copyist mentioned it.[3]
36. *Kitāb al-Wuḥdān* (The Book of Singular Reports).[4]

COMPILATION OF THE ṢAḤĪḤ

[Imām Bukhārī's magnum opus was not an ordinary compilation of ḥadīth, but it was an outcome of sixteen years of continuous scholarly effort. The following section outlines the various steps Bukhārī took in producing the *Ṣaḥīḥ*.]

Stage 1: Selecting Narrators

[Abū Bakr] al-Ḥāzimī writes,

> These scholars have specific methods for selecting the sources of ḥadīths, which we will address briefly. The methodology of those who narrate authentic reports [*ṣaḥīḥ*] is to examine the status of the upright narrator in respect to his teachers and sources, who are also reliable [*thiqah*]. His authentic well-established [*ṣaḥīḥ thābit*] ḥadīth from some of them will definitely be included. By contrast, his ḥadīth from others is defective, which will only be included as support and corroboration.

---

1 *Hudā as-Sārī*, 492.

2 *At-Tārīkh al-Kabīr*, 3:5:2. [Keeping in mind that the title of *Ṣaḥīḥ al-Bukhārī* also bears the description *al-Musnad* and that the incident under discussion is cited in the *Ṣaḥīḥ* (no. 3905/5807), it is possible that Bukhārī is referring to his *Ṣaḥīḥ*. Trans.]

3 *Hudā as-Sārī*, 492.

4 *Kashf aẓ-Ẓunūn*, 2:1469; *Hudā as-Sārī*, 492. [*Kitāb al-Wuḥdān* lists those Companions from whom only one ḥadīth is narrated. Trans.]

This is a complex matter that is understood by recognizing the ranks and merits of the students transmitting from a particular teacher. The following example illustrates this point: Zuhrī's students are of five categories, each of which is distinguished from the other. The first category is of the utmost authenticity [*al-ghāyah fī 'ṣ-ṣiḥḥah*] and is the utmost objective of Bukhārī.

The second category is the same as the first in terms of probity [*ʿadālah*]. The first category, however, combines memory [*ḥifẓ*] and precision [*itqān*] along with lengthy companionship with Zuhrī, such that among them were those who accompanied him in his travels and residence. The second category accompanied Zuhrī only for a short while and, therefore, did not develop an affinity with his ḥadīths, and they are less precise than the first category. They meet the criteria of Muslim.

The third category comprises transmitters who accompanied Zuhrī like the first category, but they are not free from the blemishes of criticism [*jarḥ*] and are, therefore, at times accepted and at times rejected. They meet the criteria of Abū Dāwūd and Nasa'ī.

The fourth category comprises transmitters who are similar to the third category in terms of criticism and accreditation [*taʿdīl*], but they lack affinity with Zuhrī's ḥadīths due to their brief exposure to him. They meet the criteria of Abū ʿĪsā [at-Tirmidhī].

The fifth category comprises weak [*ḍuʿafā'*] and unknown narrators [*majhūlīn*]. Those who compile ḥadīths based on chapters may only include their ḥadīths for consideration [*iʿtibār*] and support [*istishhād*]. They are found in [the works of] Abū Dāwūd and those with less stringent criteria, but not in [the works of] the Two Shaykhs [Bukhārī and Muslim].[1]

The first category comprises the likes of Mālik, Ibn ʿUyaynah, ʿUbaydullāh ibn ʿUmar, Yūnus al-Aylī, ʿUqayl al-Aylī, Shuʿayb ibn Abī Ḥamzah, et al. The second category comprises the likes of ʿAbd ar-Raḥmān ibn ʿAmr al-Awzāʿī, al-Layth ibn Saʿd, an-Nuʿmān ibn

1 Ḥāzimī, *Shurūṭ al-A'immah al-Khamsah*, 150–154.

> Rāshid, ʿAbd ar-Raḥmān ibn Khālid ibn Musāfir, et al. The third category comprises the likes of Sufyān ibn Ḥusayn as-Sulamī, Jaʿfar ibn Barqān, ʿAbdullāh ibn ʿUmar ibn Ḥafṣ al-ʿUmarī, Zamʿah ibn Ṣāliḥ al-Makkī, et al. The fourth category comprises the likes of Isḥāq ibn Yaḥyā al-Kalbī, Muʿāwiyah ibn Yaḥyā aṣ-Ṣadafī, Isḥāq ibn ʿAbdillāh ibn Abī Farwah al-Madanī, Ibrāhīm ibn Yazīd, al-Muthannā ibn aṣ-Ṣabbāḥ, et al. The fifth category comprises the likes of Baḥr ibn Kanīz as-Saqqā', al-Ḥakam ibn ʿAbdillāh al-Aylī, ʿAbd al-Quddūs ibn Ḥabīb ad-Dimashqī, Muḥammad ibn Saʿīd al-Maṣlūb, et al. There are many more, but I have sufficed with the aforementioned. I have written an independent book where I mentioned them in detail.
>
> At times, Bukhārī will include narrators of the second category, Muslim of the third category, and Abū Dāwūd from the prominent narrators of the fourth category based on circumstances that demand it.[1]

Commenting on Ḥāzimī's discussion, Ibn Ḥajar writes, "Bukhārī narrates from the second group predominantly in the chapter headings. Occasionally, he will narrate some ḥadīths from the third category in the chapter headings." He further writes,

> The example mentioned here pertains to the prolific transmitters. The respective students of Nāfiʿ, Aʿmash, Qatādah, et al. will be analogized accordingly. As for non-prolific transmitters, then Bukhārī and Muslim narrated their ḥadīths based on reliability, probity and infrequent error. However, if these transmitters achieved a high degree of trust [*qawī 'l-iʿtimād*], then Bukhārī and Muslim included their isolated transmission [*fard*], as is the case with Yaḥyā ibn Saʿīd al-Anṣārī. By contrast, there are those among them who are not heavily relied upon, so they included only their corroborated narrations, and that is most frequent.[2]

A Glance at Bukhārī's Criteria: I have already cited Ḥāzimī's and Ibn Ḥajar's respective remarks specifically on Bukhārī's criteria and

1 Ḥāzimī, *Shurūṭ al-A'immah al-Khamsah*, 155–156; *Hudā as-Sārī*, 9–10.
2 *Hudā as-Sārī*, 10.

methodology of including the ḥadīths of some narrators to the exclusion of others. Furthermore, Abū 'l-Faḍl Muḥammad ibn Ṭāhir al-Maqdisī writes,

> It has not been related from Bukhārī, Muslim or those who we mentioned after them that they said, "I will include in my book only that which meets such-and-such a criterion." Rather, the criteria of each one of them are deduced through a study of their books.[1]

A number of experts have cited this observation, including Mundhirī (d. 656 AH) in his treatise on criticism and accreditation,[2] Suyūṭī in *Tadrīb ar-Rāwī* and Qāsimī in *Qawāʿid at-Taḥdīth*. It is my understanding that Bukhārī ﷺ did in fact articulate some of his criteria for selecting transmitters, but those who reject the notion that Bukhārī adhered to any criteria did not take note of this. This [contention of mine] is evidenced by the following words of Tirmidhī ﷺ:

> Some scholars have criticized Ibn Abī Laylā due to his memory. Aḥmad said, "Ibn Abī Laylā's ḥadīths may not be adduced as proof." Muḥammad ibn Ismāʿīl [al-Bukhārī] said, "Ibn Abī Laylā is truthful, but I do not narrate from him because his authentic reports cannot be distinguished from the inauthentic ones. I do not narrate anything from those who are like this."[3]

Stage 2: Criteria for Writing Ḥadīths

[As quoted earlier,] Bukhārī said,

> My writing of ḥadīth was unlike that of others: If I wrote from a competent narrator, I asked him his name, agnomen, affiliation and

1 *Shurūṭ al-A'immah as-Sittah*, 85–86. [Shaykh ʿAbd al-Fattāḥ Abū Ghuddah aptly notes that there are scattered remarks related from these authors in this regard. Nonetheless, Muslim, Abū Dāwūd and Tirmidhī have written on some of the prerequisites of their compilations. Likewise, the titles of their respective works shed light on the nature of their content. Trans.]

2 *Jawāb al-Ḥāfiẓ al-Mundhirī ʿan As'ilah fī 'l-Jarḥ wa 't-Taʿdīl*, 90.

3 *Sunan at-Tirmidhī*, 2:199. [In *al-ʿIlal al-Kabīr* (p. 389), Tirmidhī relates similar remarks from Bukhārī about Zamʿah ibn Ṣāliḥ. As such, this criterion of rejecting a narrator was applied consistently. Trans.]

background in Ḥadīth. Yet if he was lacking [such competency], I requested his source-text and copied it. As for others, they care little about what they write or how they write it.[1]

Transmission from weak narrators: Therein lay the secret behind his inclusion of some weak narrators, the majority of whom were his teachers: by relying on their source-texts, he prevented their inherent weakness from affecting their narrations. Bukhārī exclusively transmitted from 435 transmitters, from whom Muslim did not transmit. Roughly 80 of them were criticized,[2] most of whom were his direct teachers and whose ḥadīths he personally analyzed.[3] Bukhārī predominantly includes their ḥadīths for corroboration and support [*shawāhid*], not as primary reports.[4] That is why experts, despite their preoccupation with critiquing the hadīths of the *Ṣaḥīḥ*, were unable to point out various types of weakness except in rare cases. Ibn Ḥajar said, "The number of these—i.e. criticized ḥadīths—in Bukhārī's book is 110, some of which Muslim also included: Muslim included 32 of these ḥadīths while Bukhārī exclusively narrated 78 ḥadīths."[5] This is Bukhārī's general methodology of transmission, from which some of his other criteria may be inferred.[6]

---

1 *Siyar Aʿlām an-Nubalāʾ*, 12:406.

2 *Fatḥ al-Mughīth*, 1:9.

3 Ibid., 1:23.

4 Ibid., 1:30.

5 *Hudā as-Sārī*, 346.

6 [*Ṣaḥīḥ al-Bukhārī* comprises various types of narrations: 1) primary ḥadīths (*uṣūl*); 2) corroborating ḥadīths (*mutābaʿāt*); 3) ḥadīths with truncated chains (*muʿallaqāt*, lit. "suspended" reports); and 4) non-Prophetic reports (*āthār*). The last two types are found in the chapter headings (*tarājim*). The requisite of authenticity (*ṣiḥḥah*) includes the primary ḥadīths, not necessarily the other categories of reports. This explanation is substantiated by the title of the *Ṣaḥīḥ*: *al-Jāmiʿ al-Musnad aṣ-Ṣaḥīḥ al-Mukhtaṣar min Umūr Rasūlillāh—ṣallallāhu ʿalayhi wa sallam—wa Sunanihi wa Ayyāmihi* (The Authentic Abridged *Musnad* Compendium of the Prophet's Affairs, Deeds and Days), which suggests that the clause of authenticity primarily applies to the *musnad* reports, i.e. Prophetic ḥadīths with continuous chains of transmission. In fact, corroborating ḥadīths will occasionally reach the level of mere soundness (*ḥasan*). See Ibn Ḥajar, *Hudā as-Sārī*, 19; ʿAwwāmah, annotations on *Tadrīb ar-Rāwī*, 2:280 and 289; cf. Brown, *Misquoting Muhammad*, 256–260.

In the prolegomenon to *Fatḥ al-Bārī*, Ḥāfiẓ Ibn Ḥajar writes that the total number

Stage 3: Selection of Material

Imam Bukhārī ﷺ frequently reflected on which material to select for his works. Muḥammad ibn Yūsuf al-Bukhārī [al-Firabrī] said, "While staying in Bukhārī's house one night, I observed that he rose and lit the lamp at least eighteen times to make notes of things that came to his mind."[1] This was also his habit when travelling. His copyist said, "During our travels, Abū ʿAbdillāh and I would share one house except during the midsummer days. He would rise fifteen to twenty times in one night, lighting a lamp each time to write ḥadīths and take notes."[2]

Stage 4: Compilation of Master Works

After an initial process of selecting sources, it appears that he would write a master work, which he would further condense into an abridged version. Then after publicizing it, he would continuously improve, omit and add to it. Ḥāfiẓ [Abū] 'l-Faḍl ibn Ṭāhir said, "Before compiling the *Ṣaḥīḥ*, Bukhārī wrote a book entitled the *Mabsūṭ* where he collected all his ḥadīths in chapters. He then searched for the most authentic ḥadīths per the outline he drafted and included them with all their routes."[3]

---

of primary ḥadīths including repetitions is 7397; suspended ḥadīths are 1341; and corroborating ḥadīths and allusions to alternative routes are 341. Thus, the total number of Prophetic ḥadīths including repetitions is 9079. This numbering does not account for non-Prophetic reports; these are 1608 in number. Therefore, the total number of reports from all categories is 10,687. The total number of ḥadīths with continuous chains excluding repetitions is 2602. Scholars have proffered different numbers of ḥadīths and reports in *Ṣaḥīḥ al-Bukhārī* via the recension of Firabrī. Ibn Ḥajar himself provides conflicting numberings. For the most part, this variation stems from a difference of methodology in counting the ḥadīths, not a substantial difference in their actual number. See Ibn Ḥajar, *Hudā as-Sārī*, 468–469 and 477; idem, *Fatḥ al-Bārī*, 13:543; ʿAwwāmah, annotations on *Tadrīb ar-Rāwī*, 2:362–369; Aʿẓamī, *Hadyat ad-Darārī li-Ṭālibī Ṣaḥīḥ al-Imām al-Bukhārī*, 153–157; Sallūm, "Introduction," in *ʿAdad Jamīʿ Ḥadīth al-Jāmiʿ aṣ-Ṣaḥīḥ*, 8. Trans.]

1 *Siyar Aʿlām an-Nubalāʾ*, 12:404.

2 Ibid. [This was quoted earlier, with the copyist identified as Muḥammad ibn Abī Ḥātim. Trans.]

3 *Taghlīq at-Taʿlīq*, 5:420.

This explanation is reinforced by Bukhārī's own practice in the *Ṣaḥīḥ*. He states,

> ʿAbdullāh ibn Ṣabbāḥ narrated to us: Muʿtamir narrated to us, saying: I heard ʿAwf say that Abū 'l-Minhāl narrated to him that he heard Abū Barzah say, "Allah will make you independent (*yughnīkum*)—or Allah elevated you (*naʿashakum*)—with Islām and Muḥammad ﷺ." Abū ʿAbdillāh said, "The word used here is *yughnīkum*, but it is supposed to be *naʿashakum*. The original of *Kitāb al-Iʿtiṣām* [chapter on Adhering to the Qurʿān and the Sunna] should be consulted."[1]

Ibn Ḥajar goes on to explain [the above in the following terms]:

> The words "The original of *Kitāb al-Iʿtiṣām* should be consulted" indicate that he authored *Kitāb al-Iʿtiṣām* independently and from there he incorporated into the *Ṣaḥīḥ* what met his criteria for the book, just as he did for *al-Adab al-Mufrad*. Noticing that this word was not what he believed to be accurate, he referred to the original, which was probably not in his possession at the time. Thus, he suggested that it be consulted and amendments be made from it."[2]

Stage 5: Multiple Revisions

After producing the first edition of a given book and teaching it to students, he would continuously improve, amend, omit and add to it. He would then reproduce the same book a second or third time—sometimes, even more than that. Bukhārī said, "I authored all my books three times."[3] Al-Muʿallimī al-Yamānī said,

> He intends [by this expression]—and Allah knows best—that he [first] authored the book and presented it to the masses. He then added to and amended his manuscript until he reproduced it a second time. He then revisited the work again, adding to and amending it, until he reproduced it a third time.

1 *Sāhīh al-Bukhārī, Kitāb al-Iʿtiṣām*, no. 7271.

2 *Fatḥ al-Bārī*, 13:246–247.

3 *Taghlīq at-Taʿlīq*, 5:318.

We can substantiate this claim in light of the various recensions of his works.

[For instance,] the *Tārīkh* is considered one of Bukhārī's earliest works, and he said, "I wrote the *Tārīkh* by the Prophet's grave during the moonlit nights."[1] He was under twenty years old at the time. So Bukhārī produced the first edition of the *Tārīkh* at an early stage of his life. That recension reached Abū Zurʿah, who noticed several oversights in the work. To explain these oversights, Ibn Abī Ḥātim ar-Rāzī authored his book *Bāyān Awhām al-Bukhārī fī Tārīkhihi* (Clarifying Bukhārī's Oversights in his *Tārīkh*). Thereafter, Bukhārī produced a second edition of his book, which was transmitted by Abū Aḥmad Muḥammad ibn Sulaymān ibn Fāris ad-Dallāl an-Naysābūrī (d. 312 AH). This was the recension that reached al-Khaṭīb al-Baghdādī [d. 463 AH]. Some of the oversights in the first edition—to which the two Rāzīs objected—were corrected. Consequently, Khaṭīb objected to them, saying, "In that book, [Ibn Abī Ḥātim] quoted things from Bukhārī that were incorrect. These were documented accurately in [another recension of] his *Tārīkh* contrary to what was related from him." Bukhārī produced a third edition of the work—transmitted by Muḥammad ibn Sahl ibn Kurdī—that contained corrections to some of the oversights Khaṭīb mentioned in his rejoinder *Muwaḍḍiḥ Awhām al-Jamʿ wa 't-Tafrīq* (Clarifying Oversights of Conflation and Distinction).[2]

From the foregoing, we learn that Bukhārī revised his books three times, as he expressly stated. We can prove this through the recensions of *at-Tārīkh al-Kabīr* and its subsequent rejoinders. We may not have multiple recensions for all of his works, but *at-Tarīkh al-Kabīr* is enough to shed light on Bukhārī's general methodology of authoring books.

1 *Siyar Aʿlām an-Nubalāʾ*, 12:400.

2 For more details, see Muʿallimī, "Introduction," in *Muwaḍḍiḥ Awhām al-Jamʿ wa 't-Tafrīq*, 1:11–12.

Stage 6: Continuous Improvements

Bukhārī constantly improved and added material to his *Tārīkh* until a late stage in his life. He said, "I authored all my books three times." He also said, "If some of the teachers of these people were brought back to life, they would not understand how I wrote the *Tārīkh* nor would they recognize it." He then said, "I revised it three times."[1] He also said, "Isḥāq ibn Rāhawayh presented my book the *Tārīkh* to ʿAbdullāh ibn Ṭāhir. He said, 'O Amīr, shall I not show you magic?' After reading it, ʿAbdullāh was impressed and said, 'I do not understand his compilation.'"[2] Isḥāq ibn Rāhawayh passed away in 230 AH. Meanwhile, in the beginning of the third volume of *at-Tārīkh al-Kabīr*, Muḥammad ibn Sahl al-Fasawī al-Muqri' mentions, "Abū ʿAbdillāh Muḥammad ibn Ismāʿīl ibn Ibrāhīm al-Bukhārī al-Juʿfī narrated to us in Basra in the year 246 AH."[3] Yet the book comprises the entries of Ḥadīth scholars and transmitters who passed away after Isḥāq ibn Rāhawayh. It even contains those who passed away after the recitation of [the work by] Muḥammad ibn Sahl in the year 246 AH. Bukhārī said, "Muḥammad ibn Bashshār Abū Bakr Bundār: he passed away in Rajab 252 AH. He heard from Ghundar.[4]

The Place of the Ṣaḥīḥ's Compilation

Opinions vary on where the *Ṣaḥīḥ* was compiled. ʿAbd al-Quddūs ibn Hammām said, "I heard many scholars say, 'Bukhārī transferred (*ḥawwal*) the chapter headings of his *Jāmiʿ* between the Prophet's grave and his pulpit. He prayed two units for every chapter heading.'"[5] Abū 'l-Faḍl Muḥammad ibn Ṭāhir al-Maqdisī related many opinions in this respect. He writes, "Bukhārī compiled his *Ṣaḥīḥ* in Bukhara," and he prefers this view. He also writes, "It is said, 'Rather, he authored

1 *Siyar Aʿlām an-Nubalā'*, 12:403.

2 *Tārīkh Baghdād*, 7:2.

3 *At-Tārīkh al-Kabīr*, 3:1:1.

4 Ibid., 1:1:49.

5 *Tahdhīb al-Asmā' wa 'l-Lughāt*, 1:74. [Ibn Ḥajar explains this statement as Bukhārī's editing the draft in order to prepare a fair copy. See *Hudā as-Sārī*, 489. Trans.]

it in Makkah in the Sacred Mosque.'" Nawawī comments on this, saying, "It is possible—rather, it is necessary—to reconcile these reports, because, as we mentioned earlier, he compiled the *Ṣaḥīḥ* over a period of 16 years. He, therefore, compiled parts in Makkah, Madīnah, Basra and Bukhara. And Allah knows best."[1]

Nawawī's explanation is supported by what Bukhārī's copyist mentioned regarding the compilation of *al-Jāmiʿ aṣ-Ṣaḥīḥ* at a later stage. He said,

> I purchased a house for 920 dirhams. Bukhārī gave me a thousand dirhams and said, "Buy your house with this money." I accepted it from him and thanked him. We then turned our focus to writing; at the time, we were busy compiling the *Jāmiʿ*. We spent the next two days compiling the *Jāmiʿ*. On that day, we wrote a substantial amount until the Ẓuhr prayer. After the Ẓuhr prayer, we continuously wrote without breaking for food. . .and then a few days passed, and we wrote again until the Ẓuhr prayer.[2]

As I have mentioned repeatedly, this was not the first time he compiled the work. Rather, he had already drafted an outline of *al-Jāmiʿ aṣ-Ṣaḥīḥ* between the Sacred Mosque of Makkah and the Prophetic grave (the most beautiful of salutations and peace be upon its inhabitant). Thereafter, he continuously omitted, added, rearranged and amended the work until his demise. As we will see in the following section, he was still in the process of improving it when he passed away.

The Original Exemplar (Aṣl) of Ṣaḥīḥ al-Bukhārī

In *Ṣaḥīḥ al-Bukhārī* it is reported that Abū Hurayrah ﷺ said, "The Prophet ﷺ said, 'The fornicator is not a believer when fornicating.'" Firabrī said, "I found in the handwriting of Abū Jaʿfar that Abū

1 Nawawī, *Talkhīṣ*, 218.

2 *Siyar Aʿlām an-Nubalāʾ*, 12:450–451.

ʿAbdillāh said, 'Its explanation is: it (i.e. faith) will be seized from him.'" Ibn Ḥajar said, "Abū Jaʿfar is Ibn Abī Ḥātim, Bukhārī's copyist."[1] It may be inferred from this passage that Firabrī was in possession of the copyist's manuscript [the exemplar of *Ṣaḥīḥ al-Bukhārī*].

In addition, Bukhārī narrates,

> ʿUmar ibn Ḥafṣ narrated to us: my father narrated to me: Aʿmash narrated to us: Ibrāhīm and aḍ-Ḍaḥḥāk al-Mashriqī narrated to us, from Abū Saʿīd al-Khudrī, who said, "The Prophet ﷺ asked his Companions, 'Is any one of you incapable of reciting a third of the Qur'ān in one night?' That was difficult for them, so they said, 'O Messenger of Allah, who among us is able to do that?' He said, '*Allāh al-Wāḥid aṣ-Ṣamad* [Sūrat al-Ikhlāṣ] is a third of the Qur'ān.'"

Firabrī said: I heard Abū Jaʿfar Muḥammad ibn Abī Ḥātim, Abū ʿAbdillāh's copyist, say: Abū ʿAbdillāh said, "This ḥadīth is narrated from Ibrāhīm via a broken chain (*mursal*) and from aḍ-Ḍaḥḥāk al-Mashriqī via a continuous chain (*musnad*)." Ibn Ḥajar writes,

> "Abū ʿAbdillāh" mentioned here is Bukhārī, the author. It seems Firabrī did not hear these words from Bukhārī directly, so he quoted them via Abū Jaʿfar. Abū Jaʿfar served as a copyist for Bukhārī; he accompanied him, knew him well, and narrated from him abundantly. Firabrī relates other useful material via Abū Jaʿfar from Bukhārī in the chapters of ḥajj, *maẓālim* [injustices], *iʿtiṣām*, and elsewhere.[2]

It follows, therefore, that Firabrī possessed a manuscript of *Ṣaḥīḥ al-Bukhārī* with handwritten annotations from Abū Jaʿfar, Bukhārī's copyist.

The Ṣaḥīḥ was Extracted from Six-Hundred Thousand Ḥadīths

Bukhārī said, "I extracted this book from a pool of six-hundred thou-

1 *Fatḥ al-Bārī*, 5:120–119.

2 Ibid., 9:60.

sand ḥadīths."[1] This claim is not farfetched.[2] Bukhārī said, "I included in this book only what is authentic. Yet I excluded other authentic ḥadīths for the purposes of brevity." Muḥammad ibn Abī Ḥātim said, "I asked Abū ʿAbdillāh, 'Do you remember everything you included in your collection?' He said, 'None of its contents escape me.'"

The Style of Ṣaḥīḥ al-Bukhārī's Original Exemplar

Abū 'l-Walīd al-Bājī said: Abū Dāwūd ʿAbd ibn Muḥammad al-Harawī related to us: Abū Isḥāq al-Mustamlī Ibrāhīm ibn Aḥmad narrated to us, saying,

> I transcribed Bukhārī's book from the original exemplar that was in Firabrī's possession. I noticed that the book was incomplete. Many places were left blank: certain chapter headings were void of content while certain ḥadīths lacked chapter headings, so we merged them together.[3]

Abū 'l-Walīd said,

> What confirms this statement is that the recensions of Abū Isḥāq al-Mustamlī, Abū Muḥammad as-Sarakhsī, Abū 'l-Haytham al-Kush-

1 *Siyar Aʿlām an-Nubalā'*, 12:402. [As the science of Ḥadīth developed, a ḥadīth began to be identified by its *isnād* and not by its text (*matn*). The growth of *isnād*s was a natural outcome of the process of transmission. So assuming that one Companion imparted a ḥadīth to five students who in turn did the same, et cetera, the number of routes would have increased exponentially. Through the process of transmission, therefore, the number of *isnād*s multiplied without an increase in the number of texts. Furthermore, apart from Prophetic ḥadīths, these large numbers comprise non-Prophetic reports as well, such as the statements and verdicts of the Companions and the Successors. See Abbott, *Studies in Arabic Literary Papyri II*, 65 ff.; Brown, *Hadith*, 219; Aʿẓamī, *Studies In Early Ḥadīth Literature*, 302–302; Abū Ghuddah, annotations on *Mabādī' ʿIlm al-Ḥadīth wa Uṣūluhu*, 55. Trans.]

2 [It is difficult to determine the exact number of individual ḥadīths. Nevertheless, Ṣāliḥ Aḥmad ash-Shāmī gathered the ḥadīths of 14 major Ḥadīth compilations: the six canonical books, *Muwaṭṭa' Mālik*, *Musnad Aḥmad*, the *Sunan*s of Dārimī and Bayhaqī, the *Ṣaḥīḥ*s of Ibn Khuzaymah and Ibn Ḥibbān, the *Mustadrak* of Ḥākim, and the *Mukhtārah* of aḍ-Ḍiyā' al-Maqdisī. In total, he gathered 114,194 ḥadīths; and after removing repetitions, there remained 28,430 ḥadīths. It should be noted that he did not regard the narration of two different Companions for an identical ḥadīth as a repetition. See Shāmī, *Maʿālim as-Sunnah an-Nabawiyyah*, 9. Trans.]

3 *At-Taʿdīl wa 't-Tajrīḥ*, 1:310.

> mīhanī and Abū Zayd al-Marwazī differ in their arrangement even though they copied from one original. That happened inasmuch as each one estimated where to place something from the margin and a scrap of paper. This will become clear to you when you find two chapter headings or more conjoined without any intervening ḥadīths.[1]

Throughout *Fatḥ al-Bārī*, Ibn Ḥajar noted scribal errors [in *Ṣaḥīḥ al-Bukhārī*]. Bukhārī placed the following chapter heading "Chapter: Protection from the Punishment of the Grave." He opens the chapter with a ḥadīth from Abū Ayyūb al-Anṣārī: "The Prophet ﷺ went out when the sun had set. He heard a sound, so he said, 'Jews who are being punished in the grave.'"[2] Ibn Ḥajar then quotes some commentators who opine that this ḥadīth is from the remainder of the previous chapter. Some scribes included it in this chapter without distinguishing between them.[3] Elsewhere Ibn Ḥajar writes, "Abū ʿAlī aṣ-Ṣadafī asserts that its mention after the ḥadīth of Ibn ʿUmar is from the doings of the scribe."[4]

In addition, Bukhārī placed the following chapter heading "Chapter: Highway Robbers are from the People of Disbelief and Apostasy." Ibn Ḥajar writes,

> His words "Chapter: Highway Robbers are from the People of Disbelief and Apostasy." This is how the chapter heading is found here according to all [the recensions]. But its placement here is problematic. I believe it was an oversight by those who transcribed Bukhārī's book from the draft.[5]

Moreover, Ibn Ḥajar related from Bulqīnī that the manuscripts of the *Ṣaḥīḥ* vary in the arrangement of the chapters. He said, "The manuscripts differ regarding the sequence of the chapter on fasting

---

1 Ibn Rushayd, *Ifādat an-Naṣīḥ*, 25–26; *Hudā as-Sārī*, 8; [al-Bājī, *at-Taʿdīl wa 't-Tajrīḥ*, 1:311. Trans.].

2 *Fatḥ al-Bārī*, 3:241.

3 Ibid., 3:242.

4 Ibid., 3:349.

5 Ibid., 12:109.

and the chapter on ḥajj. Likewise, the transmission varies in terms of their ḥadīths."[1]

The Orientalist Mingana published several folios from a manuscript of *Ṣaḥīḥ al-Bukhārī* with an extensive introduction despite his lack of familiarity. He delves into the differences in the arrangement of the *Ṣaḥīḥ*'s chapters, asking whether the chapter on fasting comes first or the chapter on ḥajj, as if he discovered a massive flaw in the book, not realizing that Hadīth scholars were well aware of this difference and clearly mentioned it in their works.[2]

Likewise, Ibn Ḥajar notes a ḥadīth that was omitted in all manuscripts apart from the manuscript read to Firabrī.[3] Be that as it may, there is no book in history that received scholarly attention, generation after generation, era after era, like Imām Bukhārī's book.

TRANSMITTERS OF THE ṢAḤĪḤ

Muḥammad ibn Ṭāhir al-Maqdisī writes, "Many people have transmitted *Ṣaḥīḥ al-Bukhārī*, such as Firabrī, Ḥammād ibn Ṣhākir, Ibrāhīm ibn Maʿqil an-Nasafī and Ṭāhir ibn Makhlad an-Nasafī."[4] Al-Amīr ibn Mākūlā writes, "The last person to transmit the *Ṣaḥīḥ* from Bukhārī was Abū Ṭalḥah Manṣūr ibn Muḥammad ibn ʿAlī al-Bazdī from the people of Bazdah. He was reliable. He passed away in 329 AH."[5] Firabrī said, "Ninety thousand people heard the *Ṣaḥīḥ* from Muḥammad ibn Ismāʿīl though no one besides me remains who narrates it."[6]

1 *Hudā as-Sārī*, 470.

2 [For an appraisal of Mingana's criticisms, see Aḥmad as-Sallūm's *Risālah fī Radd Shubah Minjānā ḥawl Ṣaḥīḥ al-Bukhārī* and Brown, *The Canonization of al-Bukhārī and Muslim*, pp. 384–386. Trans.]

3 *Fatḥ al-Bārī*, 1:153. [Ibn Ḥajar is referring to Ṣāghānī's manuscript of the *Ṣaḥīḥ*. See translator's appendix 2 for more on this manuscript. Trans.]

4 *Siyar*, 12:398.

5 *Ikmāl*, 7:243; *Siyar*, 12:398.

6 *Siyar*, 12:398. [Dhahabī does not accept Firabrī's statement quoted here. See Dhahabī, *Siyar*, 15:12. Shaykh Muḥammad ʿAwwāmah explains that his critique is unwarranted. See ʿAwwāmah, annotation on *Tadrīb ar-Rāwī*, 2:365–66. Ṣāliḥ Fatḥī explains that the words Dhahabī used here are *wa lam yaṣiḥḥ* ("it is inaccurate"), which is not a

Several recensions of the *Ṣaḥīḥ* gained prominence:

1. Abū Isḥāq Ibrāhīm ibn Maʿqil an-Nasafī al-Ḥanafī (d. 295 AH), the judge of Nasaf.

He heard [ḥadīths] from Qutaybah ibn Saʿīd and many others. He travelled extensively in the pursuit of knowledge. Dhahabī said, "He wrote *al-Musnad al-Kabīr*, *Tafsīr* and other works, and he transmitted *Ṣaḥīḥ al-Bukhārī*." Ibrāhīm ibn Maʿqil an-Nasafī al-Ḥanafī's recension has reached us via the route of Khalaf ibn Muḥammad ibn Ismāʿīl al-Khayyām (d. 361 AH). Imām Khaṭṭābī based his commentary on *Ṣaḥīḥ al-Bukhārī*, *Aʿlām al-Ḥadīth*, upon this recension. There are occasional omissions in his recension. Abū Yaʿlā al-Khalīlī said, "He is reliable (*thiqah*), a prolific memorizer (*ḥāfiẓ*)."[1]

2. Abū ʿAbdillāh al-Ḥusayn al-Maḥāmilī (235–330 AH).[2]

Bukhārī visited Baghdad many times, wherein he transmitted ḥadīths. The last person to transmit from him there was al-Ḥusayn ibn Ismāʿīl al-Maḥāmilī.[3] I have a photocopied manuscript of this

---

criticism of the chain of transmission; rather, he disagrees that Firabrī was the last to transmit the *Ṣaḥīḥ*. See Ṣāliḥ Fatḥī, "Nuskhat Ṣaḥīḥ al-Bukhārī al-Aṣliyyah wa Ashhar Riwāyātihi," *Majallat at-Turāth an-Nabawī* 1:3 (2018), 77. Trans.]

1 *Siyar*, 13:493; cf. Nasafī, *al-Qand fī ʿUlamāʾ Samarqand*, 158, and Shaykh Abū Ghuddah's annotation on *Shurūṭ al-Aʾimmah al-Khamsah*, 161. [A handful of narrations of the *Ṣaḥīḥ* via the recension of Ibrāhim ibn Maʿqil are found in secondary sources. For instance, Bayhaqī narrates, "Abū ʿAbdillāh al-Ḥāfiẓ related to us: Abū Ṣāliḥ related to me: Ibrāhīm ibn Maʿqil narrated to us: Muḥammad ibn Ismāʿīl [al-Bukhārī] narrated to us, saying: Aḥmad ibn Shabīb said: my father narrated to us, from Yūnus, who said: Ibn Shihāb said, from ʿUrwah, from ʿĀʾishah (ﷺ), who said, 'May Allah have mercy on the early emigrant women! When Allah revealed, "And they should let their headscarves fall to cover their necklines," they tore their shawls to use as headscarves.' This is how Bukhārī narrated it." See Bayhaqī, *as-Sunan al-Kubrā*, 7:142, no. 13,508; cf. Jumuʿah, *Riwāyāt al-Jāmiʿ aṣ-Ṣaḥīḥ wa Nusakhuhu*, 145–146. Trans.]

2 *Tārīkh Baghdād*, 8:19–23.

3 Ibid., 2:5. [Naẓar al-Firyābī put forward a similar claim. He bases the validity of this recension on Kirmānī's citation of a chain via Maḥāmilī in the introduction to his commentary on *Ṣaḥīḥ al-Bukhārī* as well as the presence of a manuscript that is supposedly transmitted through this chain. See Kirmānī, *al-Kawākib ad-Darārī*, 1:10; Firyābī's annotations on *Fatḥ al-Bārī*, 1:7. However, a number of experts have expressed

recension of *Ṣaḥīḥ al-Bukhārī* from the beginning until the chapter on "sudden death."

3. Abū Muḥammad Ḥammād ibn Shākir ibn Sawiyyah al-Warrāq an-Nasafī al-Ḥanafī (d. 311 AH).

He narrated from Tirmidhī and Bukhārī. He was one of the transmitters of *Ṣaḥīḥ al-Bukhārī* from its author. Bakr ibn Muḥammad ibn Jāmiʿ transmitted *Ṣaḥīḥ al-Bukhārī* from him.[1]

4. Khalaf ibn Shāhid ibn al-Ḥusayn ibn Hāshim an-Nasafī (d. 308 AH).

He transmitted *al-Jāmiʿ aṣ-Ṣaḥīḥ* from Bukhārī. The people of Samarqand heard the *Jāmiʿ* from him. He worked for the postal service there in the year 302 AH. He passed away in Rajab 308 AH.[2]

5. Abū 'l-Faḍl Ṭāhir ibn al-Ḥusayn ibn Makhlad an-Nasafī.

[Najm ad-Dīn an-Nasafī (d. 537 AH) writes:]

> He was a reliable student of Muḥammad ibn Ismāʿīl al-Bukhārī. He transmitted the *Jāmiʿ* from him. Abū Yaʿlā ʿAbd al-Muʾmin ibn Khalaf an-Nasafī, Saʿīd ibn Ibrāhīm ibn Maʿqil an-Nasafī and Muḥammad ibn Zakariyyā an-Nasafī narrated from him.
>
> Muḥammad ibn Ismāʿīl ibn Yūsuf said: my grandfather, Abū

---

reservations on the validity of Maḥāmilī's recension. Ibn Ḥajar writes that although Maḥāmilī attended a few sessions of ḥadīth during Bukhārī's final visit to Baghdad, he did not transmit the *Ṣaḥīḥ*. In fact, many people have conflated his general transmission from Bukhārī as a transmission of his *Ṣaḥīḥ*. It appears as though Ibn Ḥajar is directing these comments to Kirmānī. See *Fatḥ al-Bārī*, 1:7; Jumuʿah, *Riwāyāt*, 210–212. Trans.]

1 *Ikmāl*, 4:394; *Siyar*, 5:15; *Taqyīd*, 1:314; *Shurūṭ al-Aʾimmah al-Khamsah*, 161. [A handful of narrations of the *Ṣaḥīḥ* via the recension of Ḥammād ibn Shākir are found in secondary sources. For instance, Bayhaqī narrates, "Abū ʿAbdillāh al-Ḥāfiẓ related to us, saying: Aḥmad ibn Muḥammad an-Nasawī related to me, saying: Ḥammād ibn Shākir narrated to us: Muḥammad ibn Ismāʿīl [al-Bukhārī] narrated to us: al-Ḥasan ibn Mudrik narrated to us, saying: Yaḥyā ibn Ḥammād narrated to me: Abū ʿAwānah narrated to us, from ʿĀṣim al-Aḥwal, who said, 'I saw the Prophet's bowl in the possession of Anas. . .'" See Bayhaqī, *as-Sunan al-Kubrā*, 1:47, no. 116; cf. Jumuʿah, *Riwāyāt*, 164–69. Trans.]

2 *Qand*, 27.

ʿUthmān Saʿīd ibn Ibrāhīm ibn Maʿqil narrated to us, saying: my father, Muḥammad ibn Mūsā ibn Hudhayl, and Ṭāhir ibn al-Ḥusayn ibn Makhlad all narrated to us, saying: Muḥammad ibn Ismāʿīl al-Bukhārī narrated to us, saying: ʿAbdullāh ibn az-Zubayr al-Ḥumaydī narrated to us, saying: Sufyān ibn ʿUyaynah narrated to us, from Yaḥyā ibn Saʿīd al-Anṣārī, from Muḥammad ibn Ibrāhīm at-Taymī, who said: I heard ʿAlqamah ibn Waqqāṣ say: I heard ʿUmar ibn al-Khaṭṭāb say: the Messenger of Allah ﷺ said, "Actions are judged by intentions. Everyone will receive what they intended. Whoever migrated for Allah and His Messenger, their migration will be for Allah and His Messenger. Whoever migrated to acquire a worldly benefit or to marry a woman, their migration will be for the purpose they migrated."[1]

6. Muḥammad ibn Mūsā ibn Hudhayl.

Nasafī writes, "Abū ʿUthmān Saʿīd ibn Ibrāhīm ibn Maʿqil said: my father, Muḥammad ibn Mūsā ibn Hudhayl, and Ṭāhir ibn al-Ḥusayn ibn Makhlad all narrated to us, saying: Muḥammad ibn Ismāʿīl narrated to us [. . .]."[2]

7. Abū ʿAbdillāh Muḥammad ibn Yūsuf ibn Maṭar al-Firabrī (231–320 AH).

He heard from ʿAlī ibn Khashram and others. He heard *Ṣaḥīḥ al-Bukhārī* several times: once in the year 248 in Firabr,[3] a second time in Bukhara in 252,[4] and a third time in Firabr in the years 253, 254 and 255; the third instance was mentioned by Ghunjār in *Tārīkh Bukhārā*.[5] He was in possession of Bukhārī's original exemplar, from which his students copied. This bolstered his rank and served as a testimony to his truthfulness.[6] Ḥāfiẓ Ibn Ḥajar writes, "His recension of the

1 Ibid., 158–159.

2 Ibid., 158.

3 *Taqyīd*, 1:132; *Siyar*, 11:15.

4 *Taqyīd*, 1:132; *Siyar*, 11:15.

5 *Taqyīd*, 1:132.

6 *Ifādat an-Naṣīḥ*, 18.

Ṣaḥīḥ is the most complete."[1] The recension of Firabrī is well known, widespread and relied upon throughout the world today. Many have transmitted from Firabrī, but his most prominent students were Abū Zayd al-Marwazī the jurist, Ibn as-Sakan, Sarakhsī and Kushmīhanī.

8. Abū Ṭalḥah Manṣūr ibn Muḥammad ibn ʿAlī ibn Qarīnah al-Bazdī (d. 329 AH).

Al-Amīr Ibn Mākūlā writes, "He was reliable. He was the last to transmit *al-Jāmiʿ aṣ-Ṣaḥīḥ* from Bukhārī."[2] Al-Jaʿfar al-Mustaghfirī writes, "They criticize his transmission due to his young age at the time of audition. The book was recited to him from Ḥammād ibn Shākir's manuscript. His townsmen heard from him, and he became a destination of academic travel during his day."[3]

9. Masīḥ ibn ʿIṣmah ash-Shīrakathī an-Nasafī.

He transmitted *al-Jamiʿ aṣ-Ṣaḥīḥ* from Bukhārī. Abū 'l-Aḥwaṣ Muḥammad ibn Maslamah ad-Dihqān transmitted the work from him.[4]

10. Mahīb ibn Sulaym.[5]
11. Abū 'l-Faḍl Jaʿfar ibn Muḥammad ibn al-ʿAbbās at-Tūbanī.

[Samʿānī writes:]

> He was the chief (*dihqān*) of Tūban, and the freed slave of the leader of the believers. He was known as Jaʿfar al-Kabīr. He settled in the city of Tūban and left behind a progeny. He heard *al-Jāmiʿ aṣ-Ṣaḥīḥ* from Abū ʿAbdillāh Muḥammad ibn Ismāʿīl. They found the reading

1 *Taghlīq at-Taʿlīq*, 5:435.

2 *Ikmāl* 7:243.

3 *Siyar*, 15:279. [There is a difference of opinion on the name of Abū Ṭalḥah's ancestor: it is either Qarīnah or Muzaynah. Likewise, his affiliation is Bazdī, but "Bazdawī" is also used. Ibn Nāṣir ad-Dīn ad-Dimashqī writes, "Bazdī: an ascription to the city of Bazdah [. . .] and 'Bazdawī' is also said. From them is the long-lived Abū Ṭalḥah Manṣūr ibn Muḥammad [ibn ʿAlī] ibn Qarīnah—it is said: Muzaynah." See Dimashqī, *Tawḍīḥ al-Mushtabih*, 1:450–451; Ibn Nuqṭah, *Ikmāl al-Ikmāl*, 4:622. Trans.]

4 *Ikmāl*, 7:246.

5 Khalīlī, *Irshād*, 959.

certificate of Abū Ṭalḥah Manṣūr ibn ʿAlī ibn Muzabnah [*sic*], the chief of Bazdah, in the handwriting of Jaʿfar ibn Muḥammad al-Kabīr on the cover of the *Jamiʿ*. Based on that, his [Abū Ṭalḥah's] audition was deemed reliable according to some. Thus, he became a destination of academic travel and was the last to transmit the *Jamiʿ* from him.[1]

Transmitters from Firabrī

Ibn Rushayd mentions seven transmitters of *Ṣaḥīḥ al-Bukhārī* from Firabrī.[2] Rushāṭī said, "Firabrī is primarily relied upon in the transmission of Bukhārī's book."[3] Ibn Rushayd writes,

> Today, the recognized route to Bukhārī in the East and the West with continuous auditions is the route of Firabrī. He was in possession of Bukhārī's original exemplar, from which his students copied. This bolstered his rank and served as a testimony to his truthfulness.[4]

Droves of people heard *Ṣaḥīḥ al-Bukhārī* from Firabrī. In *Ifādat an-Naṣīḥ*, Ibn Rushayd mentions seven people who heard *Ṣaḥīḥ al-Bukhārī* from Firabrī: 1) Abū Isḥāq al-Mustamlī; 2) Abū Muḥammad al-Ḥammūyī; 3) Abū 'l-Haytham al-Kushmīhanī; 4) Abū Zayd Muḥammad ibn Aḥmad ibn ʿAbdillāh al-Marwazī, the most eminent transmitter to narrate the book from Firabrī; 5) Abū Aḥmad Muḥammad ibn Yūsuf ibn al-Makkī al-Jurjānī; 6) Abū ʿAlī Ismāʿīl ibn Abī Naṣr Muḥammad ibn Aḥmad ibn Ḥājib al-Kushānī; and 7) Saʿīd ibn ʿUthmān ibn as-Sakan al-Baghdādī, the Ḥadīth expert.[5]

The editor of *Ifādat an-Naṣīḥ*, Dr Muḥammad ibn al-Ḥabīb ibn al-Khūjah, added the following names: 1) Muḥammad ibn ʿUmar ash-Shabbūyah; 2) Abū Ḥāmid Aḥmad ibn ʿAbdillāh ibn Nuʿaym an-Nuʿaymī; 3) Muḥammad ibn Khālid al-Ḥasan Firabrī; 4) Abū Naṣr

1 Samʿānī, *Ansāb*, 3:102.
2 *Ifādat an-Naṣīḥ*, 17–18.
3 Ibid., 15.
4 Ibid., 18.
5 *Siyar*, 16:117.

Aḥmad ibn Muḥammad al-Akhsīkatī; 5) Firabrī's grandson, Aḥmad ibn ʿAbdillāh ibn Muḥammad ibn Yūsuf al-Firabrī.[1]

Dr Muḥammad Isḥāq Khān added the following names: 1) Abū Bakr Muḥammad ibn Ḥamm ibn Nāqib al-Bukhārī; 2) Abū Bakr Muḥammad ibn Aḥmad ibn Matt al-Ishtīkhanī; 3) Abū Nuʿmān Yaḥyā ibn al-Khathlānī [*sic*];[2] and 4) Abū 'l-Ḥasan ʿAlī ibn Aḥmad al-Jurjānī.

I have come across the following additional names: 1) Ismāʿīl al-Ḥājibī;[3] 2) Abū Naṣr al-Kushānī;[4] and 3) Zurārah.[5]

Therefore, the total number of documented transmitters from Firabrī is 19 Ḥadīth scholars. The most eminent is Abū Zayd al-Marwazī and the most prominent is Kushmīhanī.

[Details on] the Transmitters from Firabrī

1. Abū Isḥāq Ibrāhīm ibn Aḥmad ibn Ibrāhīm al-Balkhī al-Mustamlī (d. 376 AH).

He narrated the *Ṣaḥīḥ* from Firabrī in 314 AH. Abū Dharr ʿAbd ibn Aḥmad, ʿAbd ar-Raḥmān ibn ʿAbdillāh ibn Khālid—in Andalusia, and Ḥāfiẓ Aḥmad ibn Muḥammad ibn al-ʿAbbās al-Balkhī have narrated from him. Abū Dharr said, "He was among the reliable and precise scholars of Balkh." He passed away in 376 AH.[6]

2. Aḥmad ibn ʿAbdillāh ibn Muḥammad ibn Yūsuf al-Firabrī.

He transmitted the *Ṣaḥīḥ* from his grandfather, as mentioned in the footnotes of *Ifādat an-Naṣīḥ*.[7]

---

1 *Ifādat an-Naṣīḥ*, 21–22.

2 [Ṣāliḥ ibn Muḥammad al-Fullānī (d. 1218 AH) transmits the *Ṣaḥīḥ* via Firabrī's student, the ascetic of Samarqand, Abū Luqmān Yaḥyā ibn ʿAmmār ibn Muqbil ibn Shāhān al-Khatlānī, who lived for 143 years. The name Abū Nuʿmān Yaḥyā ibn al-Khathlānī mentioned here is a typographical error. See Fullānī, *Qatf ath-Thamar*, 40–43; Tirhutī, *al-Yāniʿ al-Janī*, 57 ff.; Jumuʿah, *Riwāyāt al-Jāmiʿ aṣ-Ṣaḥīḥ*, 316; Nadwī, *al-Farāʾid fī ʿAwālī al-Asānīd wa Ghawālī al-Fawāʾid*, 116. Trans.]

3 *Siyar*, 16:521.

4 *Ansāb*, 6:4.

5 *Taqyīd*, 1:102.

6 *Siyar Aʿlām an-Nubalāʾ*, 16:492; *an-Nujūm az-Zāhirah*, 4:161.

7 *Ifādat an-Naṣīḥ*, 23, footnote no. 85.

3. Abū Ḥāmid Aḥmad ibn ʿAbdillāh ibn Nuʿaym ibn al-Khalīl an-Nuʿaymī (d. 386 AH).[1]

He narrated from Abū 'l-ʿAbbās ad-Daghūlī, al-Ḥusayn ibn Muḥammad as-Sinjī and Ibrāhīm ibn Ḥamdawayh. He transmitted Bukhārī's *Jāmiʿ* from Firabrī. He was in his nineties when he passed away in Herat in the year 386 AH.[2]

[*] Abū Aḥmad Aḥmad ibn Muḥammad ibn Aḥmad ibn Maḥfūẓ al-Warqūdī. He transmitted *Ṣaḥīḥ al-Bukharī* from Firabrī.[3]

4. Aḥmad ibn Ḥājib ibn Muḥammad al-Kushānī (d. 392 AH) [*sic*].[4]
5. Zurārah.

In *Ṭabaqāt Ahl Shīrāz*, Muḥammad ibn ʿAbd al-ʿAzīz al-Qaṣṣār mentioned that Abū Aḥmad Muḥammad ibn Muḥammad ibn Yūsuf ibn Makkī al-Jurjānī entered Shiraz and narrated ḥadīth there. The masses, judges and reliable people gathered around him; they positioned him by the Maṣāḥif entrance and heard from him. He had authorization for *Ṣaḥīḥ al-Bukhārī* via Zurārah [*sic*], from Firabrī.[5]

---

1 Ibn Mākūlā, *Ikmāl*, 7:378.

2 *Siyar Aʿlām an-Nubalā'*, 16:488; Samʿānī, *at-Taḥbīr fī 'l-Muʿjam al-Kabīr*, 2:95.

3 *Ansāb*, 5:64 [/13:317].

4 *Ikmāl*, 7:185. [The provided reference to Ibn Mākūlā's *Ikmāl* under the entry of Kushānī does not mention Aḥmad ibn Ḥājib al-Kushānī. There is mention of his son Muḥammad and grandson Ismāʿīl, both of whom will be mentioned later in Dr Aʿẓamī's list. However, in his supplementary work to *Ikmāl* entitled *Ikmāl al-Ikmāl*, Ibn Nuqṭah provides an entry for Aḥmad ibn Ḥājib where he mentions that Aḥmad's agnomen was Abū ʿUmar, he was reliable, his son Muḥammad narrates from him, and he passed away after 330 AH. There is no mention of him transmitting the *Ṣaḥīḥ* from Firabrī. See Ibn Nuqṭah, *Ikmāl al-Ikmāl*, 3:326; cf. annotations on *Ikmāl*, 4:564. Trans.]

5 Ibn Nuqṭah, *Taqyīd*, 1:102–103. [In the mentioned reference, Ibn Nuqṭah states that Abū Aḥmad Muḥammad al-Jurjānī had authorization for *Ṣaḥīḥ al-Bukhārī* "via Zurārah, from Firabrī." No biographical information was provided for Zurārah. In his edition of *Taqyīd* (1:110 and 258), the editor Sharīf at-Tashādī notes a manuscript variant that contains the last passage as "he transmitted it via Firabrī (*rawāhu ʿan al-Firabrī*)" without any mention of Zurārah. Earlier, Aʿẓamī cited Ibn Rushayd saying that Abū Aḥmad al-Jurjānī was a direct student of Firabrī. Therefore, the name Zurārah is a scribal error. Also see Sallūm, "Introduction," in *Mukhtaṣar an-Naṣīḥ*, 69. Trans.]

6. Abū ʿAlī Saʿīd ibn ʿUthman ibn as-Sakan al-Bazzār al-Baghdādī al-Miṣrī (294–353 AH).

He heard ḥadīths in Baghdad, Harran, Damascus and Nishapur. He heard *Ṣaḥīḥ al-Bukhārī* from Muḥammad ibn Yūsuf al-Firabrī in Khurasan.[1] Towards the latter part of his life, after extensive travels, he settled down in Egypt. Earnings from business supported his extensive travels. He was the first to bring and transmit the *Ṣaḥīḥ* in Egypt. He authored many books, but they are found among the North Africans. Among his works is *Ṣaḥīḥ Ibn as-Sakan*.[2]

7. Abū Muḥammad ʿAbdullāh ibn Aḥmad ibn Ḥammūyah as-Sarakhsī (293–381 AH).

He heard *al-Musnad al-Kabīr* and the *Tafsīr* of ʿAbd ibn Ḥumayd ibn Ibrāhīm ibn Khuzaym ash-Shāshī, *Musnad ad-Dārimī* from ʿĪsā ibn ʿUmar as-Samarqandī, and Bukhārī's *al-Jāmiʿ aṣ-Ṣaḥīḥ* from Firabrī in the year 316 AH.[3] He authored a book on the number of ḥadīths in *Saḥīḥ al-Bukhārī*. Abū Dharr al-Harawī and others narrated from him. Abū Dharr said, "I recited to him; he is reliable."[4]

8. Abū 'l-Ḥasan ʿAlī ibn Aḥmad ibn ʿAbd al-ʿAzīz al-Jurjānī (d. 366 AH).[5]

He heard from ʿUmar ibn Bujayr and others, and al-Ḥākim and others narrated from him. He transmitted *al-Jāmiʿ aṣ-Ṣaḥīḥ* from Firabrī.

9. Muḥammad ibn Aḥmad ibn Ḥājib al-Kushānī ad-Dihqān.
10. Abū ʿAlī Ismāʿīl ibn Muḥammad ibn [Aḥmad ibn] Ḥājib al-Kushānī.

[Samʿānī writes:] He heard *Ṣaḥīḥ al-Bukhārī* alongside his father from Firabrī in Firabr in the year 316 AH.[6] [Dhahabī writes:] He transmitted

1 *Siyar Aʿlām an-Nubalāʾ*, 16:117.
2 Kattānī, *ar-Risālah al-Mustaṭrafah*, 23.
3 Samʿānī, *Ansāb*, 4:292–293.
4 *Siyar Aʿlām an-Nubalāʾ*, 16:292–293.
5 Sahmī, *Tārīkh Jurjān*, 276–277; *Siyar Aʿlām an-Nubalāʾ*, 16:247.
6 Samʿānī, *Ansāb*, 4:6.

Ṣaḥīḥ al-Bukhārī from Firabrī. He heard it in the year 320 AH. He was the last to narrate *Ṣaḥīḥ al-Bukhārī* with an elevated chain. Abū Sahl al-Abīwardī, Shujāʿī, ʿUmar ibn Aḥmad as-Samarqandī and others have narrated from him. Dhahabī said, "He was senior and lived a long life." Al-Mu'taman as-Sājī said, "He passed away in the year 392 AH."[1]

11. Muḥammad ibn Aḥmad ibn Matt as-Samarqandī al-Ishtīkhanī (d. 388 AH).[2]

He heard *Ṣaḥīḥ al-Bukhārī* from Firabrī in the year 319 AH. Abū Naṣr ad-Dāwūdī said,

> I visited Ibn Matt in Ishtīkhan. He asked me, "Have you heard Bukhārī's *Jāmiʿ*?" I said: "yes." He asked, "From whom?" I said, "From Ismāʿīl al-Ḥajibī." He said, "Hear it from me, because I was an adult when I heard it and he was being carried around on people's shoulders."

12. Abū Zayd Muḥammad ibn Aḥmad ibn ʿAbdillāh al-Marwazī.[3]

He was a leading Shāfiʿī jurist who travelled extensively. He heard [ḥadīths] from Aḥmad ibn Muḥammad al-Mundhirī, Muḥammad ibn ʿAbdillāh as-Saʿdī and others. He heard *Ṣaḥīḥ al-Bukhārī* from Firabrī in the year 318 AH.[4] He transmitted the *Ṣaḥīḥ* in Basra and Shiraz;[5] he sojourned in Makkah and transmitted the *Ṣaḥīḥ* there. Al-Khaṭīb al-Baghdādī said, "He was the most eminent of its transmitters."[6]

13. Abū Bakr Muḥammad ibn Ḥamm ibn Nāqib al-Bukhārī aṣ-Ṣaffār (d. 381 AH).[7]

---

1 *Siyar Aʿlām an-Nubalāʾ*, 16:481. [Ibn Nuqṭāh concurs with Dhahabī that Ismāʿīl al-Kushānī heard the *Ṣaḥīḥ* from Firabrī in the year the latter passed away, 320 AH. See Ibn Nuqṭah, *Taqyīd*, 1:407. For an example of a ḥadīth found exclusively in Ismāʿīl al-Kushānī's recension via Firabrī, see Mizzī, *Tuḥfat al-Ashrāf*, 5:222–223. Trans.]

2 *Siyar Aʿlām an-Nubalāʾ*, 16:521; Subkī, *Ṭabaqāt ash-Shāfiʿiyyah al-Kubrā*, 3:99.

3 *Siyar Aʿlām an-Nubalāʾ*, 16:313–315.

4 Ibid., 16:315.

5 Samʿānī, *Ansāb*, 3:239.

6 *Tārīkh Baghdād*, 1:314; *Ifādat an-Naṣīḥ*, 22.

7 *Siyar Aʿlām an-Nubalāʾ*, 16:424–425; Ibn Mākūlā, *Ikmāl*, 7:422.

He heard [ḥadīths] from al-Ḥusayn ibn Isma‘īl al-Fārisī and Muḥammad ibn Sa‘īd. He narrated *Ṣaḥīḥ al-Bukhārī* from Firabrī.

14. Muḥammad ibn Khālid ibn al-Ḥasan al-Firabrī.

Abū Sulaymān al-Khaṭṭābī said, "Muḥammad ibn Khālid ibn al-Ḥasan al-Firabrī narrated *al-Jāmi‘ aṣ-Ṣaḥīḥ* from Firabrī except for some ḥadīths towards the end [*sic*]."[1]

15. Abū ‘Alī Muḥammad ibn ‘Umar ibn Shabbūyah al-Marwazī (d. 296 AH).[2]

He was a senior Ṣufī mentor. He heard the *Ṣaḥīḥ* from Firabrī in 316 AH, and he transmitted it in Merv in 378 AH.

16. Abū Aḥmad Muḥammad ibn Muḥammad ibn Yūsuf al-Makkī al-Jurjānī (d. 374 AH).[3]

He travelled to the Levant and Egypt. He narrated from Baghawī, Ibn Ṣā‘id and others. He transmitted *Ṣaḥīḥ al-Bukhārī* from Firabrī in Basra and Sutrān.

17. Abū 'l-Haytham Muḥammad ibn al-Makkī ibn [Muḥammad ibn al-Makkī ibn] Zurā‘ al-Marwazī al-Kushmīhanī (d. 389AH).[4]

---

1 *Ifādat an-Naṣīḥ*, 23, footnote no. 85. [In his commentary on *Ṣaḥīḥ al-Bukhārī*, Khaṭṭābī writes that he narrates most of the *Ṣaḥīḥ* from the recension of Ibrāhīm ibn Ma‘qil "except some ḥadīths in the ending that were transmitted from Muḥammad ibn Yūsuf al-Firabrī. Muḥammad ibn Khālid ibn al-Ḥasan narrated them to me, saying: Firabrī narrated them to us." See Khaṭṭābī, *A‘lām al-Ḥadīth*, 1:106. Trans.]

2 *Siyar A‘lām an-Nubalā'*, 16:423; *Ikmāl*, 5:107–108; *Ansāb*, 7:285.

3 *Tārīkh Jurjān*, p. 427. [The editor of *Tārīkh Jurjān* writes that he was unable to locate a place called Sutrān and proposes Shiraz and Siraf. Jumu‘ah Fatḥī quotes the same passage from *Tārīkh Jurjān* but replaces the word Sutrān with Shiraz. See Jumu‘ah, *Riwāyāt*, 302. As we saw earlier, Muḥammad ibn ‘Abd al-‘Azīz al-Qaṣṣār mentioned in *Ṭabaqāt Ahl Shīrāz* that Abū Aḥmad al-Jurjānī travelled to Shiraz and transmitted the *Ṣaḥīḥ* there. Therefore, the correct word is most likely Shiraz, not Sutrān. See Ibn Nuqṭah, *Taqyīd*, 1:102–103. Trans.]

4 *Siyar A‘lām an-Nubalā'*, 16:491–492. [Ibn Rushayd writes that his ancestor's name is vowelized as Zurā‘: a *ḍammah* on the *zāy* and one *rā'*. An alternative vowelization with a *shaddah* on the *rā'* is provided in the marginal notes of the manuscript. See *Ifādat an-Naṣīḥ*, 36; Ibn Nuqṭah, *Ikmāl al-Ikmāl*, 2:649. Trans.]

He narrated from ʿAbdullāh ibn Muḥammad ibn Ibrāhīm ad-Dāghūnī and Muḥammad ibn Aḥmad ibn ʿĀṣim. He transmitted *Ṣaḥīḥ al-Bukhārī* multiple times from Firabrī. Abū Dharr al-Harawī, Karīmah al-Marwaziyyah, Abū Sahl Muḥammad ibn Aḥmad al-Hafṣī and others have narrated from him. Dhahabī said, "He was truthful (*ṣadūq*)."

Transmitters from Kushmīhanī

1. Muḥammad ibn Aḥmad ibn Muḥammad al-Ḥākim al-Muzakkī (d. 444 AH).

He heard ḥadīth in Khurasan and Makkah. He narrated from Zāhir as-Sarakhsī and Ḥaddādī.[1]

2. Abū ʿAbdillāh Muḥammad ibn ʿAlī ibn Muḥammad ibn al-Ḥasan al-Khabbāzī (d. 449 AH).

He travelled to Abū 'l-Haytham al-Kushmīhanī to hear *Ṣaḥīḥ al-Bukhārī*; he heard it from him, and it was recited to him. Yamīn ad-Dawlah Abū 'l-Qāsim Muḥammad ibn Nāṣir ad-Dīn summoned him to Ghaznah. He heard his recitation intently, hosted him and sent him to Nishapur. In his day, reliance was upon his audition and manuscript.[2]

3. Muḥammad ibn Saʿīd ibn Sakhtawayh al-Isfarāyīnī.

He resided in Makkah and passed away there. He transmitted *Ṣaḥīḥ al-Bukhārī* from Abū 'l-Haytham in Makkah.[3]

4. Muḥammad ibn ʿAbd ar-Raḥīm ibn al-Ḥasan al-Atharī al-Khubūshānī (d. c. 430 AH).

He narrated from Zāhir, Ḥaddādī and Abū Nuʿaym. He was a reliable transmitter from the experts of Ḥadīth.[4]

---

1 *Al-Muntakhab min as-Siyāq*, 39.
2 Ibid., 43.
3 Ibid., 46.
4 Ibid., 48.

5. Abū Sahl Muḥammad ibn Aḥmad ibn ʿUbaydillāh al-Ḥafṣī al-Marwazī (d. after 465 AH)

A shaykh of good repute. "He was from the laity, but he was of reliable audition." His audition of *Ṣaḥīḥ al-Bukhārī* from Kushmīhanī became known in Merv. The author of *Muntakhab* opines that Ḥafṣī was the last person to transmit the *Ṣaḥīḥ* from Kushmīhanī. Thus, the scholars of Merv heard from him. That audition earned him such honour and acceptance that he was escorted to Nishapur where Niẓām al-Mulk hosted him. The *Ṣaḥīḥ* was recited to him in the Niẓāmiyyah in a gathering also attended by the children of the judges, imams and authorities.[1]

6. Aḥmad ibn Muḥammad ibn ʿAbdillāh al-Bajalī an-Naysābūrī aṣ-Ṣūfī (362–449 AH).

He was the leading Ḥadīth expert of his day. Scholars recited to, and heard from, him in Nishapur, Isfahan, Tabaristan, the cities of Khurasan and Transoxiana.[2]

7. Abū ʿAbd ar-Raḥmān Ismāʿīl ibn Aḥmad ibn ʿAbdillāh aḍ-Ḍarīr (361-after 440 AH).

He travelled extensively in the pursuit of knowledge. He authored well-known works in the disciplines of the Qurʾān, Qurʾānic recitation and Ḥadīth.[3] Abū Bakr al-Khaṭīb recited *Ṣaḥīḥ al-Bukhārī* to him in three sittings.[4]

8. Abū Ṭāhir al-Ḥusayn ibn ʿAlī ibn al-Ḥasan al-Hamadhānī.

---

1 Ibid., 60. [Dhahabī writes that Ḥafṣī passed away in 465 AH, whereas Samʿānī writes, "I believe he passed away in 466 AH." See *Siyar*, 18:245; *Ansāb*, 2:239; Jumuʿah, *Riwāyāt*, 292. *Al-Muntakhab min as-Siyāq* is Abū Isḥāq as-Ṣarīfīnī's (d. 641 AH) abridgement of ʿAbd al-Ghaffār al-Fārisī's (d. 529 AH) *Tārīkh Naysābūr*. That Ḥafṣī was the last to transmit *Ṣaḥīḥ al-Bukhārī* from Kushmīhanī should, therefore, be ascribed to the author of *Tārīkh Naysābūr*, not the author of *Muntakhab*. Trans.]

2 *Al-Muntakhab min as-Siyāq*, 93–94.

3 Ibid., 129–130.

4 Samʿānī, *Ansāb*, 4:327.

He travelled to Nishapur to study Ḥadīth, then to Sarakhs where he wrote, and then to Kushmihan where he heard *Ṣaḥīḥ al-Bukhārī* from Abū 'l-Haytham al-Kushmīhanī.[1]

9. Al-Ḥajjāj ibn Muḥammad ibn Abī Saʿīd as-Sakhtawī al-Isfarāyīnī.

His father resided in Makkah.[2]

10. Abū ʿUthmān Saʿīd ibn Muḥammad ibn Aḥmad al-Baḥīrī al-Mulqābādhī [d. 451 AH].

A senior, reliable shaykh from a household of spirituality and uprightness. He was "from the prominent members of the Prophet's progeny and one of the Ṣūfīs." He heard the *Ṣaḥīḥ* from Kushmīhanī in Merv.[3]

11. Abū 'l-Khayr [Muḥammad] ibn Abī ʿImrān [d. 471 AH].

He was the last person to transmit *Ṣaḥīḥ al-Bukhārī* from Kushmīhanī from Firabrī.[4]

12. Abū 'l-Ḥasan al-ʿAlā' ibn Muḥammad ibn Muḥammad al-Isfarāyīnī.[5]
13. Umm al-Kirām Karīmah bint Aḥmad al-Marwaziyyah (d. 463 AH).

She resided in Makkah.[6]

---

1 *Al-Muntakhab min as-Siyāq*, 199–200.

2 Ibid., 212.

3 Ibid., 232–233.

4 *At-Taḥbīr fī 'l-Muʿjam al-Kabīr*, 2:151[cf. Samʿānī, *Ansāb*, 11:117; *Siyar*, 18:383. Earlier, we saw that ʿAbd al-Ghaffār al-Fārisī opines that Ḥafṣī was the last to transmit the *Ṣaḥīḥ* from Kushmīhanī. The difference may stem from the varying opinions on whether Abū 'l-Khayr's audition from Kushmīhanī was established. Samʿānī believed that the allegations that Abū 'l-Khayr never heard from him were unfounded. That explains why Samʿānī maintained that Abū 'l-Khayr was the last surviving student to transmit the *Ṣaḥīḥ* from Kushmīhanī. See *Siyar, op cit.*; Ibn Ḥajar *Lisān al-Mizān*, 7:540. Trans.]

5 *Al-Muntakhab min as-Siyāq*, 401.

6 Ibid., 427.

14. Abū Dharr ʿAbd ibn Aḥmad al-Harawī [d. 434 AH].[1]
15. Jaʿfar ibn Muḥammad al-Mustaghfirī [d. 430 AH].[2]

1 *Ifādat an-Naṣīḥ*, 37.
2 *Siyar Aʿlām an-Nubalā'*, 17:564.

Chapter 2

THE ROLE OF ISNĀD IN ISLAMIC CIVILIZATION

History shows that Islamic civilization is unrivaled when it comes to its attention to the transmitters of its history, books and narratives of its prophets and their exhaustive efforts in this regard. Indeed, their attention to the chains of transmission and narrators was not limited to the religious disciplines; but it also included belles-lettres, historical reports and other fields, whereby their attention to Prophetic ḥadīths was far deeper [than other people's methods] and possessed greater nuance. The Qur'ān and the Prophetic Sunna are to remain till the Day of Judgement, and so towards that end the Muslims have instituted an unprecedented system of education—unapparelled today and in the past. The foundations of this system were put in place during the Prophetic era, and rest on two fundamental principles.

The *first principle* is the transmission of knowledge via the chain of transmission (*isnād*), which entails ascribing a statement to its source or its transmitter. In his *Ṣaḥīḥ*, Imām Bukhārī mentions:

CHAPTER: THE STATEMENT OF A ḤADĪTH SCHOLAR: HE NARRATED TO US OR HE RELATED US. . .

- Abū 'l-ʿĀliyah narrated on the authority of Ibn ʿAbbās [ﷺ], from the Prophet ﷺ, from what he narrates from his Lord ﷻ.
- Anas [ﷺ] narrated on the authority of the Prophet ﷺ, who narrates from his Lord ﷻ.

- Abū Hurayrah [ﷺ] narrated on the authority of the Prophet ﷺ, who narrates from your Lord ﷻ.[1]

Abū ʿAlī al-Jayyānī said, "Allah (Exalted is He) distinguished this civilization with three unprecedented traits: *isnād*, knowledge of genealogy and desiential inflection (*iʿrāb*)."

Al-Ḥākim an-Naysābūrī said,

> Had it not been for *isnād* and scholarly insistence upon it, the lighthouse of Islam would have collapsed and the heretics and innovators would have fabricated ḥadīths and altered the chains of transmission. Undoubtedly, reports are fragmented when they are devoid of chains of transmission.
>
> Abū 'l-ʿAbbās Muḥammad ibn Yaʿqūb narrated to us, saying: al-ʿAbbās ibn Muḥammad ad-Dūrī narrated to us, saying: Abū Bakr ibn Abī 'l-Aswad narrated to us, saying: Ibrāhīm Abū Isḥāq aṭ-Ṭālqānī narrated to us, saying: Baqiyyah narrated to us, saying: ʿUtbah ibn Abī Hakīm narrated to us that he was with Isḥāq ibn Abī Farwah in the presence of Zuhrī. Ibn Abī Farwah began saying, "The Prophet ﷺ said." Zuhrī told him, "May Allah destroy you, Ibn Abī Farwah! How bold are you against Allah! Can you not mention the *isnād* for your ḥadīth? You are narrating to us ḥadīths that have no reins or bridles.[2]

This is how Ḥadīth scholars from the first generation perceived the vital status of *isnād* in the discipline of Ḥadīth, for it serves as its most important pillar and foundation vis-à-vis discussions of probity and retention. Likewise, they understood that content criticism cannot be applied accurately without an analysis of the *isnād*.[3] No statement can be authentic until its chain of transmission is established.

---

1 *Al-Jāmiʿ aṣ-Ṣaḥīḥ*, 1:22.

2 *Maʿrifat ʿUlūm al-Ḥadīth*, 6. The exchange between Zuhrī and Ibn Abī Farwah can be found in [Samʿānī's] *Adab al-Imlāʾ wa 'l-Istimlāʾ*, 5. These reports can be found *Tadrīb ar-Rāwī*, 2:605. [On the origins of Abū ʿAlī al-Jayyānī's remarks, see Shaykh ʿAwwāmah's annotations to *Tadrīb ar-Rāwī*, 4:581. Trans.]

3 [When a person says a ḥadīth has problematic content, he either believes the Prophet ﷺ himself made a problematic statement or alternatively he believes someone in the chain leading to the ḥadīth made an error in transmission. When Ḥadīth scholars

Ibn Ḥazm said,

> The transmission of reliable narrators, successively reaching back to the Prophet ﷺ, has been used by Allah to distinguish the Muslims from other sects. Interrupted and problematic chains are found among the Jews, but they do not reach [the time of] Mūsā [ﷺ] like we reach [the time of] Muḥammad ﷺ. They stop short of Mūsā's lifetime with a gap of over thirty generations. In fact, it is not possible for them to reach a Prophet's disciple or his follower.[1]

Many statements have been related from the predecessors (*salaf*) emphasizing the importance of *isnād*. Ibn al-Mubārak said, "*Isnād* is part of the religion. Were it not for *isnād*, anyone could say whatever they wanted."[2] Sufyān ibn ʿUyaynah said, "Zuhrī narrated a ḥadīth one day, so I said, 'Present it without an *isnād*.' Zuhrī said, 'Do you climb to the roof without the stairs?'" Thawrī said, "*Isnād* is the weapon of the believer."[3] Aḥmad ibn Ḥanbal said, "Seeking elevated chains is the practice of the predecessors. The students of ʿAbdullāh [ibn Masʿūd] would travel from Kufa to Madīnah to learn and hear from ʿUmar." Muḥammad ibn Aslam aṭ-Ṭūsī said, "Shortness of the *isnād* is closeness to Allah ﷻ." Muḥammad ibn Sīrīn said, "This knowledge is religion; so be wary of whom you take your religion from." He [Ibn Sīrīn] also said,

> They did not ask for *isnād* [in earlier times], but when the strife (*fitnah*)

---

found the content of a ḥadīth problematic, they would identify a flaw in the chain, as it was inconceivable that the Prophet could utter something problematic. Ibn aṣ-Ṣalāḥ has explained this idea in clear terms: "When the text of a ḥadīth (*matn*) is inauthentic, it is impossible for it to have an authentic chain." See Ibn aṣ-Ṣalāḥ, *Fatāwā Ibn aṣ-Ṣalāḥ*, 45. With this in mind, one can understand why Ḥadīth scholars primarily focused on *isnād*-based criticism, and how the content of a ḥadīth impacted their evaluation of its chain of transmission. On the primacy of *isnād* criticism, see Idlibī, *Manhaj Naqd al-Matn*, 190; Ḥasanī, *Maʿrifat Madār al-Isnād*, 1:534. Trans.]

1 [Ibn Ḥazm's remarks have been paraphrased here by Suyūṭī in *Tadrīb ar-Rāwī*. For the full version, see Ibn Ḥazm, *Fiṣal*, 2:67–70. Trans.]

2 Introduction to *Ṣaḥīḥ Muslim*, 1:12; *Sharaf Aṣḥāb al-Ḥadīth*, 41, no. 78; *Ilmāʿ*, 194.

3 Al-Khaṭīb al-Baghdādī cites it with a chain of transmission in *Sharaf Aṣḥāb al-Ḥadīth*, 42, no. 81.

> occurred, they said, "Name your sources for us: those who belong to the Ahl as-Sunnah, their ḥadīths will be accepted; and those who are innovators, their ḥadīths will be rejected."[1]

The *second principle* was the preservation of books. It was unacceptable for a scholar, however knowledgeable he may have been, to acquire a book and teach it without first acquiring a manuscript that corresponded to the original exemplar. In this regard, Imām Mālik maintained a set of prerequisites for the validity of authorization:

> The secondary copy [of the book used for authorization] should be cross-referenced with the exemplar until they are identical. In addition, the authorizer should be adept in what he is authorizing, reliable in his faith and transmission, and recognized for knowledge. Moreover, the one seeking authorization should be from the people of knowledge and characterized by it, so that knowledge is entrusted to the worthy.[2]

AUTHOR'S PERSONAL CHAIN OF TRANSMISSION

Every book, therefore, has a pedigree. For instance, the pedigree for this manuscript of *al-Jāmiʿ aṣ-Ṣaḥīḥ* as it relates to me is as follows:

> I narrate the *Ṣaḥīḥ* on the authority of many teachers. The most prom-

1 [There is considerable debate on the interpretation of *fitnah* in the words of Ibn Sīrīn. Some scholars opine that it refers to the assassination of ʿUthmān ibn ʿAffān ﷺ. See Qurṭubī, *Mufhim*, 1:123; Abū Ghuddah, *Lamaḥāt*, 73. Based on a statement of Ibrāhīm an-Nakhaʿī that people only began asking for *isnād* during the era al-Mukhtār ibn Abī ʿUbayd ath-Thaqafī (d. 67 AH), some argue for a later date. See Aḥmad, *al-ʿIlal wa Maʿrifat ar-Rijāl*, 3:380; ʿAwwāmah, annotations on *Tadrīb ar-Rāwī*, 3:160. With variations on the specific date, many contemporary scholars agree that the fabrication of ḥadīths began around the year 40 AH. Mujīr al-Khaṭīb explains that fabrication began during the period of the Successors when the first wave of internal conflicts and innovations surfaced. Therefore, it is preferable to leave the date unspecified so as to include the various opinions. See Ḥasanī, *Maʿrifat Madār al-Isnād*, 1:385. Trans.]

2 Qāḍī ʿIyāḍ, *Ilmāʿ*, 95. Qāḍī ʿIyāḍ maintains that the first two conditions [i.e. cross-referencing the manuscript and reliability of the authorizer] are necessary vis-à-vis audition, presentation and authorization. However, the third condition [i.e. status of the student] is disputed.

inent among them, I believe, is our teacher Maulana Husain Ahmad Madani. We completed *al-Jāmiʿ aṣ-Ṣaḥīḥ* through audition (*samāʿ*) and presentation (*ʿarḍ*) over one academic year in 1371 AH/1951–1952 CE.

He narrates from *Shaykh al-Islām* Maulana Maḥmūd al-Ḥasan ad-Deobandī—who was held captive in Malta by the British—from Shaykh ʿAbd ar-Raḥmān al-Pānipatī, from Shāh Muḥamamd Isḥāq ad-Dihlawī, from Shāh ʿAbd al-ʿAzīz ad-Dihlawī, from Shāh Walī Allah ad-Dihlawī, [who said]: Shaykh Abū Ṭāhir Muḥammad ibn Ibrāhīm al-Kurdī al-Madanī related to us, saying: my father Shaykh Ibrāhīm al-Kurdī al-Madanī informed us, saying: I read to Shaykh Aḥmad al-Qushāshī, who said: Aḥmad ibn ʿAbd al-Quddūs Abū 'l-Mawāhib ash-Shinnnāwī related to us, saying: Shaykh Shams ad-Dīn Muḥammad ibn Aḥmad ibn Muḥammad ar-Ramlī informed us, on the authority of Shaykh Zakariyyā ibn Muḥammad Abū Yaḥyā al-Anṣārī, who said: I recited to Shaykh Ḥāfiẓ Abū 'l-Faḍl Shihāb ad-Dīn Aḥmad ibn ʿAlī ibn Ḥajar al-ʿAsqalānī, from Ibrāhīm ibn Aḥmad at-Tanūkhī, from Abū 'l-ʿAbbās Aḥmad ibn Abī Ṭālib al-Ḥajjār, from al-Ḥusayn ibn al-Mubārak az-Zabīdī, from Shaykh Abū 'l-Waqt ʿAbd al-Awwal ibn ʿĪsā ibn Shuʿayb as-Sijzī al-Harawī, from Shaykh Abū 'l-Ḥasan ʿAbd ar-Raḥmān ibn Muẓaffar ad-Dāwūdī, from Abū Muḥammad ʿAbdullāh ibn Aḥmad as-Sarakhsī, from Abū ʿAbdillāh Muḥammad ibn Yūsuf ibn Maṭar ibn Ṣāliḥ ibn Bishr al-Firabrī, from Imām Bukhārī.

In addition, many friends and family narrate from us—and from others—via continuous chains of transmission until the scholars of Ḥadīth. I would like to mention in particular the eminent scholar Niẓām al-Yaʿqūbī, who narrates the *Ṣaḥīḥ* on the authority of:

(a) His long-lived teacher, the great transmitter, ʿAbd al-Qayyūm ibn Zaynillāh al-Bastawī ar-Raḥmānī—partly through recitation and the remainder through transference (*munāwalah*) coupled with authorization—who narrates it from his teacher Aḥmadullāh al-Partāpgarhī ad-Dihlawī, from the polymath, the great transmitter of India, Nadhīr Ḥusayn ad-Dihlawī, *ḥā* (transition)—

(b) He [Yaʿqūbī] also narrates it through a complete audition from his teacher, the great transmitter, the jurist, the wise, Muḥammad Isrā'īl ibn Muḥammad Ibrāhīm an-Nadwī, who said: (i) ʿAbd al-Jabbār ash-Shakrāwī informed us: ʿAbd al-Wahhāb al-Multānī and Aḥmadullāh al-Partāpgarhī ad-Dihlawī, *ḥā* (transition)—And I [Nadwī] recited, with an elevated chain, portions from the beginning and the end to (ii) ʿAbd al-Ḥakīm al-Jaywarī, who authorized me. All three [ʿAbd al-Wahhāb, Aḥmadullāh and ʿAbd al-Ḥakīm] said: Nadhīr Ḥusayn related to us, saying:

Shāh Muḥammad Isḥāq ad-Dihlawī related to us, saying: Shāh ʿAbd al-ʿAzīz ibn Walī-Allāh ad-Dihlawī related to us: my father related to us through audition until the chapter of ḥajj and the remainder was completed under his successors: Abū Ṭāhir al-Kūrānī related to us: Ḥasan al-ʿUjaymī related to us: ʿĪsā ath-Thaʿālibī al-Jaʿfarī related to us: Sulṭān al-Mazzāḥī related to us: Aḥmad ibn Khalīl as-Subkī related to us: an-Najm Muḥammad al-Ghayṭī related to us:

(a) Qāḍī Zakariyyā al-Anṣārī related to us: Ibrāhīm ibn Ṣadaqah al-Ḥanbalī related to us: ʿAbd al-Wahhāb ibn Razīn al-Ḥamawī, *ḥā* (transition)—

(b) Qāḍī Zakariyyā said: Aḥmad ibn ʿAlī ibn Ḥajar al-ʿAsqalānī related to us through audition for a substantial portion and through authorization: Ibrāhīm ibn Aḥmad at-Tanūkhī al-Baʿlī informed us.

He [Ibrāhīm at-Tanūkhī] and Ibn Razīn [al-Ḥamawī] said: Aḥmad ibn Abī Ṭālib al-Ḥajjār—Ibn Razīn added: and Sitt al-Wuzarā' Wazīrah bint ʿUmar at-Tanūkhiyyah—both related to us, saying: al-Ḥusayn ibn al-Mubārak az-Zabīdī related to us: Abū 'l-Waqt ʿAbd al-Awwal ibn ʿĪsā as-Sijzī al-Harawī related to us: ʿAbd ar-Raḥmān ibn Muḥammad ad-Dāwūdī al-Būshanjī related to us: ʿAbdullāh ibn Aḥmad ibn Ḥammūyah as-Sarakhsī related to us: Muḥammad ibn Yūsuf ibn Maṭar al-Firabrī related to us: Muḥammad ibn Ismāʿīl al-Bukhārī related to us twice.

[I would also like to mention] Shaykh Naẓar al-Firyābī, who has an extensive Ḥadīth curriculum vitae (*thabat*), and our dear Ramaḍān Aḥmad ʿAlī ʿAwf al-Miṣrī, who narrates from his teacher Muṣṭafā

Abū Sulaymān an-Nadwī ash-Shāfiʿī al-Ḥusaynī—his name is ʿAbd al-Karīm ibn as-Sayyid al-Badawī Aḥmad ibn Sulayman al-Ḥusaynī.

In 2003, I founded a centre for Ḥadīth in Turkey with 30 male and female students, the majority of whom held PhDs. Today—[namely] 2011, so that is within eight years—that number exceeds 1,000 male and female students, the majority of whom hold degrees of higher studies, who transmit [Ḥadīth] books according to the methods laid out by the Ḥadīth scholars. All praise is for Allah, and it is all with His favour!

Chapter 3

THE YŪNĪNIYYAH: THE MOST PROMINENT MANUSCRIPT OF ṢAḤĪḤ AL-BUKHĀRĪ

The *Yūnīniyyah* manuscript of *Ṣaḥīḥ al-Bukhārī* has gained universal acclaim for features that would capture the interest of any serious seeker of sacred knowledge. It is ascribed to the scholar who edited it in light of multiple recensions of *Ṣaḥīḥ al-Bukhārī*: Sharaf ad-Dīn ʿAlī ibn Muḥammad ibn Aḥmad ibn ʿAbdillāh ibn ʿĪsā Abū ʾl-Ḥusayn al-Yūnīnī al-Baʿlabakkī al-Ḥanbalī. He was a scholarly authority, a Ḥadīth expert, a jurist, a mufti, unparalleled, an ascetic, a remnant of the predecessors, and the leader among his peers. He was born on 11 Rajab 621 AH in Yūnīn, a city in Baalbek.[1] He was martyred in 701 AH.[2]

ḤĀFIẒ YŪNĪNĪ'S CURRICULUM VITAE

Acquisition of Knowledge: In his hometown Baalbek, he attended sessions on a number of treatises with al-Bahāʾ ʿAbd ar-Raḥmān ibn Ibrāhīm ibn Aḥmad al-Maqdisī. He also studied with ʿAbd al-Wāḥid ibn Abī al-Maḍāʾ al-Irbilī, Ibn Rawāḥah, his father and others.

He frequented Damascus where he heard from Ibn az-Zabīdī,

1 [Although the town is famously known as Yūnīn, it also takes the name Yūnān. See Zabīdī, *Tāj al-ʿArūs*, 36:14. Trans.]

2 [On Friday 5 Ramaḍān 701 AH, after entering a local library, Yūnīnī was physically assaulted by a deranged assailant. This attack eventually led to his demise several days later at the age of 80. See Dhahabī, *Muʿjam ash-Shuyūkh al-Kabīr*, 2:40; Ibn Rajab, *Dhayl Ṭabaqāt al-Ḥanābilah*, 4:332. Trans.]

[Ibn] al-Lattī, Ibn aṣ-Ṣalāḥ, Jaʿfar al-Hamadānī, Mukram ibn Abī 'ṣ-Ṣaqar, Ibn ash-Shīrāzī and others. After the age of 40, he travelled to Egypt in the pursuit of further knowledge and Ḥadīth. There he heard from Ibn al-Jummayzī ʿAlī ibn Hibatillāh al-Lakhmī, Ibn Rawāj ʿAbd al-Wahhāb ibn Ẓāfir ibn ʿAlī, as-Sāwī Yūsuf ibn Maḥmūd and others. He travelled to Egypt five times. He stayed in the company of Zakī ad-Dīn ʿAbd al-ʿAẓīm ibn ʿAbd al-Qawī al-Mundhirī, completing his training under him.

He heard Abū 'l-Faraj ibn al-Jawzī's *Manāqib al-Imām Aḥmad* from al-Bahā' ʿAbd ar-Raḥmān ibn Ibrāhīm ibn Aḥmad al-Maqdisī, who heard it from the author. He heard *Ṣaḥīḥ al-Bukhārī* from Abū ʿAbdillāh al-Ḥusayn ibn al-Mubārak ibn az-Zabidī al-Baghdādī; and he was the most outstanding transmitter of the book from the latter. He heard *Musnad ʿAbd ibn Ḥumayd* from Abū 'l-Munajjā ʿAbdullāh ibn ʿUmar ibn al-Lattī.[1]

Teachers: Muḥammad ibn Abī 'l-Fatḥ ibn Abī 'l-Faḍl al-Baʿlabakki, the son-in-law of Sharaf ad-Dīn [al-Yūnīnī], wrote a *mashyakhah* (catalogue of teachers) for him in thirteen parts. Only the 8th to 10th parts have reached us, which mention 26 teachers.[2] Likewise, Yūnīnī's son has a *mashyakhah* that was prepared by Muḥammad ibn Yaḥyā al-Maqdisī al-Ḥanbalī (d. 759 AH), in which he dedicated the fifteenth entry to his father [Yūnīnī].[3]

Scholarly Praise

His brother, al-Quṭb Mūsā (d. 711 AH), said, "He was an eminent scholar, well-versed in Ḥadīth, lexicography and syntax. He had handsome features and a neat appearance, particularly when conducting Ḥadīth auditions. He was 80 years old."[4]

Birzālī (d. 739 AH) said,

1 *Dhayl at-Taqyīd li-Maʿrifat Ruwāt as-Sunan wa 'l-Masānīd*, 3:172.

2 Muḥammad ibn al-Faḍl al-Baʿlabakkī, *Mashyakhat Sharaf ad-Dīn*, ed. Dr. ʿUmar ʿAbd as-Salām Tadmurī.

3 *Mashyakhat al-Imām Muḥyī ad-Dīn ʿAbd al-Qādir ibn ʿAlī al-Yūnīnī al-Baʿlabakkī*, 87.

4 *Dhayl Mir'āt az-Zamān*, 1:665.

> He was an eminent scholar, handsome, graceful, striking in appearance, and poised. He was a man of great virtue. He memorized many ḥadīths and understood their meanings, was well-versed in language, articulate and well-spoken. People admired him, and he, in return, showed them great affection. He fulfilled the rights of people and held them in high esteem. He was very generous to those visiting his hometown."[1]

Dhahabī made a number of statements about him: "He was a venerable scholar with a radiant countenance. He was good company, resourceful and qualified in many fields. He was joyful and disarmingly humble."[2] "He possessed many noble traits, and he was illuminated in appearance and awe-inspiring."[3] "He was religious, knowledgeable, joyful, compassionate, a possessor of many noble traits and unparalleled."[4] "He was well-versed with the rules of transmission, possessed sharp comprehension, together with being learned in nomenclature and narrators."[5] "He was an authority, a Ḥadīth expert, immaculate, a jurist, a mufti, well-versed in language and obscure words, highly resourceful, methodical, revered by kings and leaders, awe-inspiring, humble, joyful, and good company, giving everyone their due rights."[6]

Ṣafadī (d. 764 AH) said, "He was good company, generous, pious, awe-inspiring and had handsome features."[7]

Ḥāfiẓ Ibn Kathīr (d. 774 AH) said, "He was devout, committed and composed."[8]

At-Taqī al-Fāsī (d. 832 AH), "He was well-versed in Ḥadīth, known

1 *Al-Muqaffā ʿalā Kitāb ar-Rawḍatayn*, 3:183–184.

2 *Muʿjam ash-Shuyūkh*, 2:40.

3 *Al-Muʿjam al-Mukhtaṣṣ*, 168.

4 *Dhayl Tārīkh al-Islām*, 18.

5 *Tadhkirat al-Ḥuffāẓ*, 4:1500.

6 Ibn Rajab, *Dhayl Ṭabaqāt al-Ḥanābilah*, 4:332. Ibn Rajab frequently quotes *Siyar Aʿlām an-Nubalāʾ*.

7 *Al-Wāfī bi 'l-Wafayāt*, 21:421. These are the words of Dhahabī.

8 *Al-Bidāyah wa 'n-Nihāyah*, 18:13.

for his memory; he was acquainted with jurisprudence and other fields. People admired him."[1]

Ḥāfiẓ Ibn Ḥajar (d. 852 AH) said, "He was well-versed in lexicography, memorized many texts, well-versed in the chains of transmission, the leading scholar of his town, and a destination for academic travel."[2]

Suyūṭī (d. 911 AH) said, "He was well-versed in the rules of transmission, deeply perceptive, learned in the texts and narrators [of ḥadīths], and dedicated to Ḥadīth and its harmonization (*ḍabṭ*)."[3]

Al-Ḥasan ibn ʿUmar ibn al-Ḥasan ad-Dimashqī (d. 779 AH) said, "He was noble, eminent, handsome, striking in appearance, articulate, affectionate and admired by people."[4]

His Scholarly Attention to al-Jāmiʿ aṣ-Ṣaḥīḥ

Ḥāfiẓ Yūnīnī afforded great scholarly care to *al-Jāmiʿ aṣ-Ṣaḥīḥ*. He was deeply immersed in it, assiduous in vowelizing and amending it, and meticulous in cross-referencing it with reliable manuscripts that were transmitted by experts. Ḥāfiẓ Dhahabī said,

> He informed me that he cross-referenced the *Ṣaḥīḥ* in one year and dictated it eleven times, reciting it himself. He frequently reproduced it in his own writing. In addition, he developed deep juristic insight, issued verdicts, taught, and achieved expertise in a number of disciplines.

He also said, "He had someone transcribe the *Ṣaḥīḥ*. He then refined it with several manuscripts, cross-referenced it many times, and then recited to Ibn Mālik [. . .] the book and its words. Thus, his teacher Ibn Mālik heard it from him."[5]

At-Taqī al-Fāsī (d. 832 AH) said, "He heard *Ṣaḥīḥ al-Bukhārī* from Abū ʿAbdillāh al-Ḥusayn ibn al-Mubārak ibn az-Zabīdī al-Baghdādī;

---

1 *Dhayl at-Taqyīd li-Maʿrifat Ruwāt as-Sunan wa 'l-Masānīd*, 3:172.

2 *Ad-Durar al-Kāminah*, 3:98.

3 *Ṭabaqāt al-Ḥuffāẓ*, 520.

4 *Tadhkirat at-Tanbīh fī Ayyām al-Manṣūr wa Banīh*, 1:242.

5 *Dhayl Tārīkh al-Islām*, 18, no. 6.

and he was the most outstanding transmitter to narrate the book from the latter."

Ḥāfiẓ Ibn Ḥajar (d. 852 AH) said, "He read *Bukhārī* to Ibn Mālik in order to make amendments, while Ibn Mālik heard it from him for transmission and shared linguistic points with him."

The great historian Nuwayrī (d. 733 AH) said,

> He afforded scholarly care to *Ṣaḥīḥ al-Bukhārī* with all its routes. He thoroughly refined his manuscript, assigning a symbol for each route, and wrote accurate annotations on the work. I transcribed *Ṣaḥīḥ al-Bukhārī* from his manuscript seven times. I refined it like he refined it, and I cross-referenced it with his exemplar. That was the manuscript I used for my audition with Ḥajjār and Wazīrah.[1]

THE YŪNĪNIYYAH MANUSCRIPT

Ḥāfiẓ Yūnīnī's dedication to harmonizing the recensions of *al-Jāmiʿ aṣ-Ṣaḥīḥ,* by cross-referencing and refining them,[2] was accomplished through reliance upon four important manuscripts:

1. A manuscript read to Abū Dharr al-Harawī via the route of Abū

---

1 *Nihāyat al-Arab*, 32:17.

2 [In the introduction to his manuscript, Yūnīnī explains that the mother-text for the cross-analysis was copied by Ibn Zayd (d. 702 AH) from the manuscript used for the authorization he received from his teacher Abū ʿAbdillāh al-Ḥusayn az-Zabīdī in the citadel of Damascus in the year 630 AH. Abū Hāshim al-ʿUtaybī argues that the mother-text was copied from ʿAbd al-Ghanī al-Maqdisī's manuscript, which in turn was copied from Abū 'l-Waqt's manuscript and contained variants from other recensions. Based on the attendance signatures on Maqdisī's manuscript, ʿUtaybī continues, it is clear that this was the manuscript Zabīdī utilized in 630 AH when teaching Yūnīnī. Hence, Zabīdī's authorization of *Ṣaḥīḥ al-Bukhārī* described in Yūnīnī's introduction was based on Maqdisī's manuscript; therefore, it was the source of the mother-text. See ʿUtaybī, *Kitāb Jabr*, 68, 122, 163 and 401; cf. Jumuʿah, *Riwāyāt*, 678. Since Zabīdī was authorized by Abū 'l-Waqt, for him to use Maqdisī's manuscript—instead of the manuscript he used when studying under Abū 'l-Waqt—was not an issue because Maqdisī's manuscript was copied from Abū 'l-Waqt's manuscript. Until the 9th century AH, Maqdisī's manuscript was the most authoritative for the Levantines, with reading signatures from Mundhirī (d. 656 AH), Dhahabī and ʿAlā'ī (d. 761 AH). Trans.]

'l-ʿAbbās Aḥmad ibn al-Ḥuṭay'ah, who was originally from Fez and then migrated to Egypt.[1]

2. A manuscript read to Aṣīlī, annotated by Ibn ʿAbd al-Barr Yūsuf ibn ʿAbdillāh an-Namarī al-Qurṭubī.[2]
3. The manuscript used for the audition of Abū 'l-Qāsim ibn ʿAsākir ʿAlī ibn al-Ḥusayn ad-Dimashqī, the historian of the Levant, which was missing the 13th and 33rd parts.[3]
4. A manuscript read to Abū 'l-Waqt ʿAbd al-Awwal ibn ʿĪsā as-Sijzī al-Harawī.[4]

Sharaf ad-Dīn al-Yūnīnī thoroughly cross-referenced these manuscripts under the supervision of the celebrated authority Ibn Mālik Muḥammad ibn ʿAbdillāh aṭ-Ṭā'ī al-Jayyānī, who had settled in Damascus. This [process] was conducted in the presence of eminent Ḥadīth experts, who followed along with reliable manuscripts of *al-Jāmiʿ aṣ-Ṣaḥīḥ*. When they came across passages that appeared to conflict with conventional laws of Arabic grammar, Ibn Mālik would ask whether the narration was transmitted in that manner. If they responded in the affirmative, he would explicate the passage within his capacity. Whenever he selected, preferred or suggested an amendment, Yūnīnī would immediately amend his manuscript and mark it as authentic. In an instance when there were two or three desinential inflections (*iʿrāb*), Yūnīnī annotated as he was advised and preferred accordingly. They proceeded in this fashion until the

1 [He used the symbol *hā'* for this manuscript. Given that Abū Dharr narrates via Mustamlī (d. 376 AH), Ḥammūyah (d. 381 AH) and Kushmīhanī (d. 389 AH) from Firabrī, further symbols distinguish the source of the variant. Trans.]

2 [Via Abū Zayd al-Marwazī (d. 371 AH) from Firabrī, for which he used the symbol *ṣād*. Trans.]

3 [Via multiple routes leading back to Firabrī, for which he used the symbol *sīn*. Trans.]

4 [This was the manuscript of Abū Saʿd as-Samʿānī (d. 562 AH) via Abū 'l-Waqt (d. 553 AH) via Dāwūdī (d. 467 AH) via Ḥammūyah from Firabrī, for which he used the symbol *ẓā'*, interestingly on account of Samʿānī's precision and phenomenal memory (*ḥifẓ*). This manuscript was also read to Karīmah al-Marwaziyyah (d. 463 AH) via Kushmīhanī from Firabrī. As such, it contains both the variants of Abū 'l-Waqt and Karīmah al-Marwaziyyah. See ʿUtaybī, *Kitāb Jabr*, 150; Jumuʿah, *Riwāyāt*, 673 and 679. Trans.]

cross-referencing and amendments were completed in the 71st session. In relation to this, Ibn Mālik wrote his book *Shawāhid at-Tawḍīḥ wa 't-Taṣḥīḥ li-Mushkilāt al-Jāmiʿ aṣ-Ṣaḥīḥ*.[1]

Yūnīnī functioned as the teacher and reciter while Ibn Mālik—who was 20 years older than him—attended as a student, listener and transmitter. In terms of transmission and audition, this was the practice of the pious predecessors in studying from reliable, qualified teachers even if the student was older than the teacher. Nonetheless, Yūnīnī also sat as a student, benefitting from Ibn Mālik in terms of language, explication and amendments to the text of the *Ṣaḥīḥ*.[2] In the introduction to *Irshād as-Sārī*,[3] Qasṭallānī dated this audition to the year 676 AH.[4]

1 *Qabas min ʿAṭā' al-Makhṭūṭ al-ʿArabī*, 1:114. [It is clear from a close reading of *Shawāhid at-Tawḍīḥ* and his comments noted in the margins of Yūnīnī's manuscript that Ibn Mālik did not alter any alleged grammatical errors in the text of *Ṣaḥīḥ al-Bukhārī*. He only vowelized and explicated abstruse passages. Yet even with regards to passages that ostensibly conflicted with conventional grammar laws, if they were established as being part of the reliable transmission, then he simply provided explanations for them rather than merely rejecting them on grammatical grounds. That being said, very few passages ostensibly conflicted with conventional grammar laws, in his estimation. In many instances, he simply presented the grammatical origins of passages that already conformed to these laws, highlighted points of disagreement among grammarians, and used certain passages as a pretext to elucidate concepts that were not adequately addressed in other books. See Ṭāhā Muḥsin, "Introduction," in *Shawāhid at-Tawḍīḥ*, 15–16. Trans.]

2 From the article of the Ḥadīth expert, the erudite scholar, Shaykh Aḥmad Shākir printed in the introduction of the Dār al-Jīl edition of *al-Jāmiʿ aṣ-Ṣaḥīḥ*.

3 *Irshād as-Sārī*, 1:40.

4 Aḥmad Shākir writes, "In *Irshād as-Sārī*, it is dated to the year 676 AH. Qasṭallānī spelled it out in letters: *sitt wa sabʿīn wa sitt miʾah* (six-hundred and seventy-six), not numbers [in which case, there was a greater chance of a typographical error]. This is definitely a mistake, because Ibn Mālik passed away in 672 AH. At first, I thought it was a typographical error. I then consulted the manuscripts of Qasṭallānī's commentary at the Egyptian National Library. I found the date written like the printed edition, so I was convinced that the mistake was from the author, who made an oversight at the time of writing. The correct date is possibly 666 AH or 667 AH; hence, the source Qasṭallānī quoted had it written as *sitt wa sittīn*, but he read *sitt wa sabʿīn* and quoted it as such. Alternatively, it was written as 667, but when he quoted it, he read a seven in between the two identical numbers [i.e. six]. Allah knows best the accuracy of this [explanation]. I exerted considerable effort in trying to determine the correct date. However, I could not find anything mentioned explicitly in the extant sources.

SECONDARY COPIES

Scholars have transcribed multiple manuscripts based on Yūnīnī's manuscript of *al-Jāmiʿ aṣ-Ṣaḥīḥ*, which they used for cross-referencing and amendments. They labelled these manuscripts as secondary (*furūʿ*), because they were cross-referenced and amended according to Yūnīnī's manuscript. Rightfully so, they regarded Yūnīnī's manuscript as the exemplar and the ultimate criterion. In what follows, we will present only three prominent secondary copies.

First: Ghazūlī's handwritten manuscript

He is Shams ad-Dīn Muḥammad ibn Aḥmad ibn Ṣafī ibn Qāsim ibn ʿAbd ar-Raḥmān aṣ-Ṣūfī. He was born in Ramaḍān 697 AH and passed away in the early part of 777 AH.[1] In the introduction to *Irshād as-Sārī*, Qasṭallānī writes,

> I came across several secondary copies of this master exemplar. In my estimation, the most outstanding of them is the notable secondary copy—possibly superior to the original: the copy attributed to the authority, the Ḥadīth expert, Shams ad-Dīn Muḥammad ibn Aḥmad al-Mizzī al-Ghazūlī, which was endowed to the Tankiziyyah by the Maḥrūq entrance outside Cairo. It was cross-referenced multiple times with two copies endowed to the madrasah of Ḥājj Mālik and Yūnīnī's exemplar, such that nothing was omitted. I, therefore, relied on Ghazūlī's copy to transcribe the text of *Bukhārī* in my commentary. I consulted it for diacritizing and vowelizing the text and the chain of every ḥadīth while noting the variant recensions and important notes found in the marginalia.

Based on the Khadawiyyah Library catalogue printed in 1310 AH/1892 CE, Ustādh Manūnī argues that the 2nd half of Ghazūlī's manuscript can be found in the Egyptian National Library. The truth of the matter, however, is this manuscript has been relocated and its whereabouts

1 In *ad-Durar al-Kāminah* (3:319, no. 859), Ibn Ḥajar wrote a biographical entry for him, quoted by at-Taqī al-Fāsī in *Dhayl at-Taqyīd*, 1:71, no. 23.

are unknown. During one of my visits to the Egyptian National Library over 25 years ago, I asked to see this manuscript. Instead, an ordinary manuscript—unrelated to Ghazūlī's or Yūnīnī's respective manuscripts—was brought. Ghazūlī's manuscript was probably misplaced or lost.

Second: The handwritten copy of ʿAbdullāh ibn Sālim al-Baṣrī

He was born in 1049 AH and passed away in 1124 AH. He spent twenty years in transcribing and refining his manuscript, relying on Yūnīnī's exemplar and other manuscripts. As such, the Baṣrī manuscript conforms to a high standard of accuracy. It became the master exemplar for subsequent prominent manuscripts. The Ḥadīth expert Muḥammad ʿAbd al-Ḥayy al-Kattānī details the whereabouts of this manuscript in the following terms:

> In the Illuminated Madīnah, I saw ʿAbdullāh ibn Sālim al-Baṣrī's handwritten manuscript of the *Ṣaḥīḥ* in eight parts in the possession of the great transmitter, the wise, Shaykh Ṭāhir Sunbul. It was of the utmost accuracy, cross-referencing and precision, and it was neatly written. He told me that he took it to Turkey to amend the Amīrī manuscript of the *Ṣaḥīḥ* that was being printed there and was later distributed by Sultan ʿAbd al-Ḥamīd [II] in the masjids and throughout the world. It was harmonized upon this. I am unsure how the manuscript came to be in his family's possession.[1]

Third: The handwritten manuscript of Nuwayrī

He is Aḥmad ibn ʿAbd al-Wahhāb ibn Muḥammad ibn ʿAbd ad-Dā'im ibn Munajjā ibn ʿAlī ibn Ṭirād ibn Ḥaṭṭāb ibn Naṣīr ibn Ismāʿīl ibn Ibrāhīm ibn Jaʿfar ibn Hilāl ibn al-Ḥusayn ibn Layth ibn Ṭalḥah ibn ʿAbdillāh ibn ʿAbd ar-Raḥmān ibn Abī Bakr aṣ-Ṣiddīq ʿAbdillāh ibn ʿAtīq, the Companion of the Prophet ﷺ: [also known as] Shihāb ad-Dīn Abū 'l-ʿAbbās al-Bakrī an-Nuwayrī ash-Shāfiʿī. He was born

1 *Fahras al-Fahāris*, 1:199.

on Wednesday night on 26 Dhū 'l-Qaʿdah 677 AH and passed away in 733 AH.

In *ad-Durar al-Kāminah*, Ḥāfiẓ Ibn Ḥajar said,

> Aḥmad ibn ʿAbd al-Wahhāb ibn Muḥammad ibn ʿAbd ad-Dā'im an-Nuwayrī Shihāb ad-Dīn. He heard [ḥadīths] from Sharīf Mūsā ibn ʿAlī ibn Abī Ṭālib, Yaʿqūb al-Hadhabānī, Bint al-Munajjā and others. He transcribed eight manuscripts of the *Ṣaḥīḥ*. He would transcribe a manuscript, cross-reference it, add the audition certificates[1] and then sell it for 1,000 [dirhams]. He compiled a voluminous history in his own handwriting in 30 volumes, which he sold for 2,000 dirhams.

Citing Birzālī, Ibn al-Jazarī said,

> He transcribed *Ṣaḥīḥ al-Bukhārī* eight times. He heard it being recited to [Bint] ibn al-Munajjā and Ibn ash-Shiḥnah. He had beautiful handwriting and was well spoken. He would cross reference a manuscript, bind it, add the audition certificates and then sell it for 700 dirhams, and at other times for 1,000 dirhams.[2]

Nuwayrī's handwritten manuscript is preserved in the Köprülü Library, Istanbul, as item no. 362 from the endowments of Fāḍil ibn Aḥmad Pāshā.

---

1 [During an audition of a Ḥadīth book, an invigilator was appointed to document the names of the attendees in a register known as a *ṭabaqah* (pl. *ṭibāq*). This register contained further information, such as the date and location of the audition and the condition of each attendee during the class. It was then kept in a masjid or a madrasah to serve as proof for the authorization of anyone who claimed to have heard the book, or the lack thereof. Abū ʿAmr ibn aṣ-Ṣalāḥ (d. 643 AH) dictated Abū Bakr al-Bayhaqī's multi-volume compendium *as-Sunan al-Kubrā* to a congregation of scholars over 757 sessions. The following are some of the points that were noted in the register after he dictated the eighth volume: the number of sessions held; personal details of the attendees (e.g. names, lineages and honorifics); the state of the attendees (e.g. who spoke during the dictation); the date of completion; the venue; and the name of the registrar. See Muḥammad Duhmān, "Introduction," in *al-Qalā'id al-Jawhariyyah fī Tārīkh aṣ-Ṣāliḥiyyah*, 1:21–22; Abū Ghuddah, *Ṣafḥah Mushriqah*, 103 and 137–138; the addendum to the 8th volume of *as-Sunan al-Kubrā* (the Hyderabad Deccan edition), 346–50. Trans.]

2 [Ibn al-Jazarī, *Tārīkh Ḥawādith az-Zamān*, 2:646, no. 799. Trans.]

The Sulṭāniyyah Edition

Sultan ʿAbd al-Ḥamīd [II] issued an imperial order for the printing of the *Ṣaḥīḥ* by Maṭbaʿah Amīriyyah, Būlāq, in 1311 AH/1893 CE.[1] The publishing house began work that very year. The first impression was completed in nine volumes in the beginning of the two Rabīʿs 1313 AH/1895 CE. In their preface, the editors explain that they relied upon an extremely precise and accurate secondary manuscript of the *Yūnīniyyah*—the reference point for the recensions of *Ṣaḥīḥ al-Bukhārī*—and another manuscript celebrated for its accuracy and precision. They did not, however, detail any other manuscript that they may have used. But a close study of their edition reveals that they also used Qasṭallānī's commentary. Furthermore, toward the end, they indicate that they were also in possession of ʿAbdullāh ibn Sālim al-Baṣrī's manuscript.

Sultan ʿAbd al-Ḥamīd [II] also issued an imperial order to the scholars of Azhar to form a committee of scholars who were deeply immersed in the field of Ḥadīth to revise the print after its editing by the publishing house. The Grand Shaykh of Azhar at the time, Ḥassūnah an-Nawāwī, gathered sixteen scholars who cross-referenced the printed edition of the *Ṣaḥīḥ* with the *Yūnīniyyah*, which was sent by the Grand Vizier Ghāzī Aḥmad Mukhtār Pāshā, who served as the Ottoman High Commissioner in Egypt.[2] Shaykh Aḥmad Shākir writes,

> It is understood from the remarks of *Shaykh al-Islām* Ḥassūnah an-Nawāwī on 20 Ṣafar 1313 AH—found in the preface to the Ṣulṭāniyyah edition—that Yūnīnī's exemplar is stored in the Istanbul Imperial Library. It was sent to the scholars of Azhar for the purposes

1 [Al-Maṭbaʿah al-Amīriyyah was opened in 1820 CE in Būlāq, a district in Cairo, under the auspices of Muḥammad ʿAlī Pāshā, the Ottoman Khedive of Egypt. Ownership of the press shifted over the decades as did the name. Prominent names include Maṭbaʿat Būlāq and Maṭbaʿat al-ʿĀmirah. See Iḥsānoghlū, *al-Atrāk fī Miṣr wa Turāthuhum ath-Thaqāfī*, 427–28. Trans.]

2 From the article of the Ḥadīth expert, the erudite scholar, Shaykh Aḥmad Shākir, who quotes the remarks of the scholars of Azhar found in the preface to the *Ṣaḥīḥ*, 2–3.

> of revision with his excellency ʿAbd as-Salām Pāshā al-Muwayliḥī. Most probably this manuscript was returned to its original place in the Istanbul Imperial Library.[1]

He further states,

> The quoted remarks from Shaykh Ḥassūnah's preface give the impression that the print was based on the *Yūnīniyyah* itself, whereas the remarks of the editors of the Sulṭāniyyah indicate that the print was based on a secondary copy. I am unable to say with certainty the correctness of either view until the manuscript used for printing resurfaces and we learn the whereabouts of the *Yūnīniyyah*—if Allah enables researchers to find it.[2]

An Overview of the [Sulṭāniyyah] Edition

First, this edition of the *Ṣaḥīḥ* does not detail its chain of transmission to Imām Bukhārī ﷺ. As established earlier, it is clear to everyone that *isnād* is an exclusive accomplishment of Islamic civilization and that it holds an important rank in the religion. The importance Ḥadīth scholars gave to *isnād* in the acceptance of transmitted knowledge led to its requirement for the acceptance of all Islamic disciplines, like Qurʾānic exegesis, jurisprudence, history, narrator criticism, genealogy, lexicography, syntax, belles-lettres, poetry and stories. The case is similar with books written in this period where they have reached us via the chains of their transmitters, even if the number of

---

1 Ibid. [During and after Yūnīnī's lifetime, his manuscript was accessible and countless secondary copies were written. It was then transferred as an endowment to the Mamluk official ʿAlāʾ ad-Dīn Aqbughā's (d. 843 AH) madrasah in Cairo, during which time Qasṭallānī (d. 923 AH) used it for his commentary on the *Ṣaḥīḥ*, entitled *Irshād as-Sārī*. After remaining in the possession of Muḥammad ar-Rūdānī (d. 1094 AH), the author of *Jamʿ al-Fawāʾid*, it passed into the hands of the Meccan Ḥadīth expert ʿAbdullāh ibn Sālim al-Baṣrī (d. 1134 AH). See Manūnī, "Ṣaḥīḥ al-Bukhārī fī 'd-Dirāsāt al-Maghribiyyah," *Majjallat al-Lughah al-ʿArabiyyah* 29 (1394 AH), 533; ʿUtaybī, *Kitāb Jabr*, 231–32. Trans.]

2 Ibid. [Ṣalāḥ Fatḥī succinctly summarizes the various opinions, concluding that they definitely did not use the original *Yūnīniyyah*; rather, they relied upon important secondary sources like ʿAbdullāh al-Baṣrī's manuscript. See Ṣalāḥ Fatḥī, *Taḥrīr al-Aṣl al-Muʿtamad fī 'ṭ-Ṭabʿah as-Sulṭāniyyah*, 15. Trans.]

transmitters for a particular book was widespread. In fact, scholars regard this as a bona fide requirement for accepting these books and establishing their ascription to their respective authors. In fact, the slogan in transmitting manuscripts was "Chains of transmission are the pedigrees of books."[1] The application of nuanced principles of transmission and meticulous adherence to the various phrases of reception that indicate the manner of audition and transmission of books are the most effective academic tools for safeguarding books from alteration.[2]

Departing from the unflinching adherence of Ḥadīth scholars to unbroken chains, the scholars who produced this valuable edition have omitted one of its most fundamental underpinnings: citing the unbroken chain of transmission until Bukhārī in the beginning of the manuscript. This omission has left writers on this edition bewildered.

Second, the scholarly adherence to citing *isnād* was even transferred to the commentators of Ḥadīth books. Thus, Shams ad-Dīn Muḥammad ibn Yūsuf al-Kirmānī (d. 786 AH),[3] Sirāj ad-Dīn ibn al-Mulaqqin (d. 804 AH),[4] Ḥāfiẓ Ibn Ḥajar al-ʿAsqalānī (d. 852 AH),[5] Badr ad-Dīn Maḥmūd ibn Aḥmad al-ʿAynī (d. 855 AH)[6] and Shihāb ad-Dīn Abū 'l-ʿAbbās Aḥmad al-Qasṭallānī (d. 923 AH)[7] cite their chains of transmission to Imām Bukhārī in the introduction to their respective commentaries before commencing their discussions, due to the importance of the successive chain leading back to the compiler.

Third, the manuscript [of *Ṣaḥīḥ al-Bukhārī*] that we are presenting to the readers is from "The High Mawlawī Sayyidī Mālikī Makhdūmī Ṣāḥibī Library—may Allāh populate it with the perpetuation of its owner," as noted on the cover page.[8] It is a secondary copy of the

1 *Fatḥ al-Bārī*, 1:5.

2 *Tawthīq an-Nuṣūṣ wa Ḍabṭihā ʿind al-Muḥaddithīn*, 27–28.

3 *Al-Kawākib ad-Darārī*, 1:2–4.

4 *At-Tawḍīḥ li-Sharḥ al-Jāmiʿ aṣ-Ṣaḥīḥ*, 1:56–57.

5 *Fatḥ al-Bārī*, 1:5.

6 *ʿUmdat al-Qārī*, 1:22–23.

7 *Irshād as-Sārī*, 1:69.

8 [This possibly refers to the library of the Ṣāḥibī Bahā'ī Madrasah founded by the

master exemplar, written by the great historian Nuwayrī. It is the 5th of seven—as Nuwayrī explicitly states, or eight as others state—manuscripts that he had written. This is the chain of transmission cited in the beginning of the book:

> It was related to us by the two long-lived great Damascene transmitters: (i) Shihāb ad-Dīn Abū 'l-ʿAbbās Aḥmad ibn Abī Ṭālib ibn Abī 'n-Niʿam Niʿmah ibn Ḥasan ibn ʿAlī ibn Bayān ibn ash-Shiḥnah al-Ḥajjār aṣ-Ṣāliḥī and (ii) the descendant of scholars, Sitt al-Wuzarā' Umm Muḥammad Wazīrah, daughter of the knowledgeable authority, Shaykh Shams ad-Dīn Abū Ḥafṣ ʿUmar, son of the erudite authority and judge, Wajīh ad-Dīn Asʿad ibn al-Munajjā at-Tanūkhī—through recitation to them as I listened in the Manṣūriyyah located in the Bayn al-Qaṣrayn district, Islamic Cairo, in Jumādā al-Ūlā during the months of 715 AH.
>
> They [Ḥajjār and Sitt al-Wuzarā'] said: Shaykh Sirāj ad-Dīn Abū ʿAbdillāh al-Ḥusayn ibn al-Mubārak ibn Muḥammad ibn Yaḥyā az-Zabīdī narrated to us in Shawwāl 630 AH, in the Muẓaffarī Mosque on Mount Qasiyun, Damascus:
>
> Abū 'l-Waqt ʿAbd al-Awwal ibn ʿĪsā ibn Shuʿayb ibn Isḥāq ibn Ibrāhīm as-Sijzī aṣ-Ṣūfī al-Harawī, related to us through recitation to him as we listened in Baghdad in the latter part of 552 AH and the beginning of 553 AH:
>
> Imām Jamāl al-Islām Abū 'l-Ḥasan ʿAbd ar-Raḥmān ibn Muḥammad ibn al-Muẓaffar ibn Muḥammad ibn Dāwūd ibn Aḥmad ibn Muʿādh ibn Sahl ibn al-Ḥakam ad-Dāwūdī related to you through recitation to him in Pushang in Dhū 'l-Qaʿdah 465 AH:
>
> Imām Abū Muḥammad ʿAbdullāh ibn Aḥmad ibn Ḥammūyah ibn Aḥmad ibn Yūsuf ibn Aʿyan as-Sarakhsī related to us through recitation to him in Ṣafar 381 AH:

---

vizier Ṣāḥib Bahā' ad-Dīn (d. 677 AH) in 654 AH. Maqrizī writes that this madarsah was the greatest institution of learning in Egypt, if not in the world, and was celebrated for its extensive library. See Maqrīzī, *al-Mawāʿiẓ wa 'l-Iʿtibār*, 4:211; Maʿṣarānī, "Tajalliyāt al-Jamāl fī Nuskhat al-Jāmiʿ aṣ-Ṣaḥīḥ li 'l-Bukhārī bi-Khaṭṭ an-Nuwayrī: Dirāsah wa Taḥqīq," *Majallat at-Turāth an-Nabawī* 1:3 (2018), 29–30. Trans.]

Imām Abū ʿAbdillāh Muḥammad ibn Yūsuf ibn Maṭar ibn Ṣāliḥ ibn Bishr ibn Ibrāhīm al-Bukharī al-Firabrī related to us in Firabr in the year 316 AH:

Imām Abū ʿAbdillāh Muḥammad ibn Ismāʿīl ibn Ibrāhīm ibn al-Mughīrah ibn al-Aḥnaf (a client of the Juʿfīs) al-Bukhārī related to us in Firabr in 248 AH once and again in [2]52 AH.

Fourth, the title of the *Ṣaḥīḥ* found on the printed manuscripts of the work does not correspond to the title designated by Imām Bukhārī. The current title is an abbreviation, perhaps by a transmitter or a scribe, and the publishing houses simply followed suit for the purposes of brevity. Imām Nawawī writes, "As for its title, then its author, Abū ʿAbdillāh al-Bukhārī, named it *al-Jāmiʿ aṣ-Ṣaḥīḥ al-Mukhtaṣar al-Musnad min Umūr Rasūlillāh—ṣallallāhu ʿalayhi wa sallam—wa Sunanihi wa Ayyāmihi*.'"[1] This title has been expressly mentioned in this manuscript:

Kitāb al-Jāmiʿ aṣ-Ṣaḥīḥ al-Mukhtaṣar al-Musnad min Umūr Rasūlillāh—ṣallallāhu ʿalayhi wa sallam—wa Sunanihi wa Ayyāmihi.

Compiled by Imām Abū ʿAbdillāh Muḥammad ibn Ismāʿīl ibn Ibrāhīm ibn al-Mughīrah ibn al-Aḥnaf al-Juʿfī al-Bukhārī ﷺ, via the transmission of Abū ʿAbdillāh Muḥammad ibn Yūsuf ibn Maṭar al-Firabrī, via Abū Muḥammad ʿAbdullāh ibn Aḥmad ibn Ḥammūyah as-Sarakhsī, via Abū 'l-Ḥasan ʿAbd ar-Raḥmān ibn Muḥammad ibn al-Muẓaffar ad-Dāwūdī, via Abū 'l-Waqt ʿAbd al-Awwal ibn ʿĪsā ibn Shuʿayb as-Sijzī al-Harawī, via Abū ʿAbdillāh al-Ḥusayn ibn al-Mubārak ibn Muḥammad ibn Yaḥyā az-Zabīdī, via Abū 'l-Ḥusayn al-Yūnīnī, Abū 'l-ʿAbbās Aḥmad ibn Abī Ṭālib al-Ḥajjār aṣ-Ṣāliḥī, Sitt al-Wuzarā' Umm Muḥammad Wazīrah bint ʿUmar ibn Asʿad ibn al-Munajjā at-Tanūkhī and others.

1 *At-Talkhīṣ Sharḥ al-Jāmiʿ aṣ-Ṣaḥīḥ*, 1:213. [On the title of *Ṣaḥīḥ al-Bukhārī*, see Abū Ghuddah, *Taḥqīq Ismay aṣ-Ṣaḥīḥayn wa Ism Jāmiʿ at-Tirmidhī*, 9–12 and 66–75. One of the earliest extant manuscripts of *Ṣaḥīḥ al-Bukhārī* from the recension of Abū Zayd al-Marwazī via Firabrī written in the 5th century bears the title *al-Jāmiʿ aṣ-Ṣaḥīḥ al-Musnad min Ḥadīth Rasūlillāh—ṣallallāhu ʿalayhi wa sallam—wa Sunanihi.* See Sallūm, "Introduction," in *al-Mukhtaṣar an-Naṣīḥ*, 76. Trans.]

This passage clarifies the title of the book as designated by Imām Bukhārī ﷺ. A gross alteration was made in the title during the first print and it continued until the present day. This passage also clarifies the transmitters of the book from Ḥāfiẓ Yūnīnī, Ḥajjār and Sitt al-Wuzarā' until Imām Bukhārī.

Fifth, the value of the handwritten manuscript [i.e. Nuwayrī's manuscript] lies in the prominence of its scribe and the appended audition certificates. The *Yūnīniyyah* is distinguished from other well-known manuscripts by these traits, the mention of the date of its transcription and appended audition certificates. Evidence for this is found in the end of the manuscript in the handwriting of the great historian Nuwayrī:

> Its transcription was completed on the blessed Saturday 20 Jumādā al-Ūlā 725 AH. Written for himself by the neediest of creation for Allah's mercy: Aḥmad ibn ʿAbd al-Wahhāb ibn Muḥammad ibn ʿAbd ad-Dā'im ibn Munajjā ibn ʿAlī ibn Ṭirād ibn Ḥaṭṭāb ibn Naṣīr ibn Ismāʿīl ibn Ibrāhīm ibn Jaʿfar ibn Hilāl ibn al-Ḥusayn ibn Layth ibn Ṭalḥah ibn ʿAbdillāh ibn ʿAbd ar-Raḥmān ibn Abī Bakr aṣ-Ṣiddīq ʿAbdillāh ibn ʿAtīq, the Companion of the Prophet ﷺ. . .
>
> This scribe is known as Nuwayrī. May Allah pardon him, be kind with him, and forgive him through His kindness and clemency! This is his 5th handwritten copy of Abū ʿAbdillāh al-Bukhārī's *al-Jamiʿ aṣ-Ṣaḥīḥ*—for Allah alone are all praise and benefaction!

From this passage, we learn the name of the scribe, the year of its transcription and its numbering; he transcribed *al-Jāmiʿ aṣ-Ṣaḥīḥ* seven times, as he mentions in *Nihāyat al-Arab*.

IMĀM NUWAYRĪ'S MANUSCRIPT

With Allah's help, we came across an invaluable manuscript of *al-Jāmiʿ aṣ-Ṣaḥīḥ* beautifully written by the pen of a scholar, jurist, lexicographer, belletrist, historian, scribe and [ḥadīth] audition-registrar, who was celebrated among scholars for accurate writing and comprehension. As noted earlier, it is said that his manuscripts were sold for 1,000 dirhams a piece owing to their precision and quality. How could this not be so when the scribe is Imām Shihāb ad-Dīn Aḥmad ibn ʿAbd al-Wahhāb al-Bakrī an-Nuwayrī, author of the encyclopedic compendium *Nihāyat al-Arab fī Funūn al-Adab*.

In the entry of Imām Yūnīnī, Nuwayrī described his own manuscript of the *Ṣaḥīḥ* ﷺ:

> He afforded scholarly care to *Ṣaḥīḥ al-Bukhārī* with all its routes. He thoroughly refined his manuscript, assigning a symbol for each route and wrote accurate annotations on the work. I transcribed *Ṣaḥīḥ al-Bukhārī* from his manuscript seven times. I refined it like he refined it, and I cross-referenced it with his exemplar. That was the manuscript I used for my audition with Ḥajjār and Wazīrah.[1]

This manuscript is decorated with useful notes and corrections penned by Ḥāfiẓ Yūnīnī from the invaluable comments of Qāḍī ʿIyāḍ, Abū ʿAlī al-Ghassānī, Ibn Mālik and other critical, meticulous scholars ﷺ.

Description of the Manuscript

This manuscript is complete and written in diacritized Naskh script, containing 298 sheets each sized 32 cm x 35 cm with 35 lines per page. The chapters and sub-chapters are written in red as well as the numbers, notwithstanding errors therein.

It [the *Yūnīniyyah*] was read by senior Ḥadīth experts to the two great transmitters of the world: Ibn ash-Shiḥnah al-Ḥajjār and Sitt al-Wuzarāʾ Umm Muḥammad.[2] The senior Ḥadīth experts who have read this manuscript include:

1. Nūr ad-Dīn al-Hāshimī [d. 725 AH].
2. Ibn Sayyid an-Nās al-Yaʿmurī [d. 734 AH].

1 *Nihāyat al-Arab*, 32:8.

2 [As we have seen in Nuwayrī's chain of transmission, in 715 AH Ḥajjār and Sitt al-Wuzarāʾ held an audition of the *Ṣaḥīḥ* in the Manṣūriyyah in Cairo. Also see Maʿṣarānī, "Tajalliyāt al-Jamāl," 18. Trans.]

3. ʿAlī ibn ʿUthmān ibn at-Turkumānī [d. 750 AH], who read from his own manuscript [during the audition where the *Yūnīniyyah* was used].
4. Athīr ad-Dīn Abū Ḥayyān al-Andalūsī [d. 745 AH].
5. Taqī ad-Dīn as-Subkī [d. 757 AH].
6. Fakhr ad-Dīn al-Muqātilī [d. 717 AH].
7. Jamāl ad-Dīn aṣ-Ṣābūnī [d. 731 AH].
8. Shihāb ad-Dīn ibn al-Bābā [d. 749 AH].

In addition, there is Ḥāfiẓ ʿIrāqī [d. 806 AH], Ḥāfiẓ Haythamī [d. 807 AH] and others.[1]

Reading Certificates[2]

1. It was completed through audition in the citadel with recitation by. . . to *Shaykh al-Islām* Ḥāfiẓ Zayn ad-Dīn al-ʿIrāqī.[3]

1 [Dr A'ẓamī prepared this list based on the reading signatures found throughout Nuwayrī's manuscript. As will be explained shortly, however, some of the signatures were written on the original *Yūnīniyah* and later appended by Nuwayrī to his own manuscript while other reading signatures were written for Nuwayrī's manuscript. Therefore, some of the scholars listed here read the *Yūnīniyyah* (e.g. Ibn Sayyid an-Nās) and others read Nuwayrī's manuscript (e.g. ʿIrāqī). Trans.]

2 [At first blush, reading certificates and registers that are appended to Ḥadīth manuscripts may seem insignificant. However, they can play an important role in literature preservation, establishing authorization and providing a snapshot of history. Based on information detailed in manuscript notes and reading certificates, a recent study restructured a micro-history of the reading sessions of Ibn ʿAsākir's (d. 571 AH) mammoth *Tārīkh Madīnat Dimashq* in Damascus, determining thereby "the background of individual participants in terms of cultural milieu, social position and status." See Konrad Hirschler, *The Written Word in the Medieval Period*, 33; Abū Ghuddah, *Ṣafḥah Mushriqah*, 79 and 146. Trans.]

3 [As alluded to earlier, some of the reading certificates written on Nuwayrī's 5th manuscript of the *Ṣaḥīḥ* do not reflect the audition of this specific manuscript. This is clear from the fact that the manuscript was transcribed in 725 AH but contains reading signatures from Ibn Sayyid an-Nās dated to 715 AH, for instance. When transcribing his manuscripts from the *Yūnīniyyah*, Nuwayrī had also transcribed the appended reading certificates found on the *Yūnīniyyah* as well as those found on ʿAbd al-Ghanī al-Maqdisī's manuscript, the *Yūnīniyyah*'s exemplar. He even asked the original signatories to re-sign his copy in order to preserve their certificates in their own handwriting. See ʿUtaybī, *Kitāb Jabr*, 158–159 and 182–192; cf. Saʿīd al-Jūmānī, "Ṣūrat al-Ijāzāt al-Manqūlah fī 'l-Makhṭūṭāt al-ʿArabiyyah," *Journal of Islamic Manuscripts* 9 (2018), 85; Maʿṣarānī, "Tajalliyāt al-Jamāl," 15–19. Trans.]

2. Aḥmad al-Ushmūnī completed it through recitation to *Shaykh al-Islām*, the erudite, Zayn ad-Dīn ʿAbd ar-Raḥīm [in 37 sessions, the last of which was in the citadel. . .].
3. It was completed through recitation in the 23rd session in al-Bustān al-Karīmī on 29 Rabīʿ al-Ākhir [7]15 AH, to the two Shaykhs [Ḥajjār and Wazīrah]—all praise is for Allah!
4. Then it was completed through recitation a second time specifically to Shaykh Abū ʾl-ʿAbbās ibn ash-Shiḥnah [al-Ḥajjār] in the citadel in the 21st session on 3 Ramaḍān 723 AH. Signed by Muḥammad ibn Muḥammad ibn Sayyid an-Nās Abū ʾl-Fatḥ al-Yaʿmurī—all praise is for Allah!
5. It was completed through recitation from his manuscript in the 18th session by the Nāṣirī entrance in Egypt, on 16 Jumādā al-Ākhirah 715 AH. It was then completed through recitation from his manuscript in the 18th session also on 16 Rajab in the year. . . Signed by ʿAlī ibn ʿUthmān al-Māridīnī, praising Allah and sending salutations upon His Prophet.
6. Aḥmad ibn ʿUthmān al-Kulūtātī completed the entire book through recitation to *Shaykh al-Islām* Zayn ad-Dīn al-ʿIrāqī.
7. Aḥmad ibn al-Kulūtātī completed the entire book with the erudite scholar Burhān ad-Dīn al-Abnāsī in his spiritual lodge in 785 AH.
8. Aḥmad ibn al-Kulūtātī completed it through recitation to *Shaykh al-Islām* [Jamāl ad-Dīn] ibn al-Bulqīnī in the year 821 AH.
9. It was completed through recitation to the authority Shaykh Ḥāfiẓ ibn Muḥammad al-Makkī al-Qurashī with another manuscript from the beginning of the book until the chapter on the obligation of zakat, and with this manuscript from the obligation of zakat until the end of the book over a number of sessions [the last being on Thursday Ṣafar 770 AH. Signed by Muḥammad ibn ash-Sharābīshī].
10. It was completed through audition in the 23rd to Najm ad-Dīn ʿAbd ar-Raḥīm [ibn Razīn with the recitation of Muḥammad ibn ʿAbdillāh] ibn Ẓahīrah al-Makkī [in Egypt].

11. It was completed through audition to the four teachers: Ibrāhīm ash-Shāmī, in its entirety. . . al-Ḥāfiz al-Ḥujjah ʿAbd ar-Raḥīm al-ʿIrāqī, Ḥāfiẓ Nūr [ad-Dīn] al-Haythamī, Ḥāfiẓ Muḥammad ad-Dijawī—seeking help [from Allah] and [for] the believers. Signed by al-Muḥibb ibn Abī ʾl-ʿAbbās.
12. Aḥmad ibn al-Manṣūr al-Ushmūnī completed through recitation to *Shaykh al-Islām*, the learned, the erudite, Zayn ad-Dīn [. . .] in 35 sessions, the last being the eighth [*sic*].[1]

End of *al-Jāmiʿ aṣ-Ṣaḥīḥ li-Umūr Rasūlillāh—ṣallallāhu ʿalayhi wa sallam—wa Sunanihi wa Ayyāmihi*, compilation of the authority, the Ḥadīth expert, Abū ʿAbdillāh Muḥammad ibn Ismāʿīl ibn Ibrāhīm—may Allah have mercy on him, be pleased with him and grant him Paradise!

1 [There are audition signatures written throughout Nuwayrī's 5th manuscript that are not listed here. Maʿṣarānī lists 112 signatures scattered throughout the entire manuscript; yet he reminds the readers that he purposely omitted some of the signatures. See *op. cit.*, 39–64. The ellipses here from Dr Aʿẓamī indicate illegible passages in the manuscript, some of which I have filled by reading the manuscript itself and ʿUtaybī's *Kitāb Jabr*. Trans.]

Appendices

Author's Appendix

Imām Bukhārī narrates over two thirds of the ḥadīths in his *Ṣaḥīḥ* from nine Companions. The following chart illustrates the percentage of ḥadīth from each of these Companions. Abū Hurayrah, for instance, narrates 1,049 ḥadīth, which is 14.3% of the overall ḥadīth in the *Ṣaḥīḥ*.

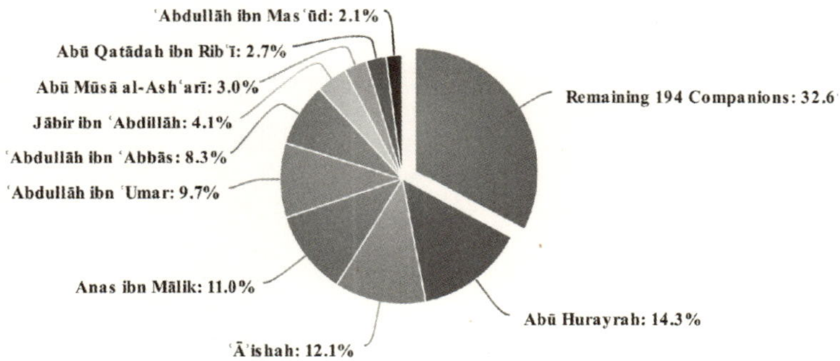

Translator's Appendix 1

MUḤAMMAD IBN YŪSUF AL-FIRABRĪ

Abū ʿAbdillāh Muḥammad ibn Yūsuf al-Firabrī was born in Firabr—a town that lay a parasang north of the Oxus on the road to Bukhara—in the year 231 AH.[1] Celebrated as one of Bukhārī's last surviving students, he played a pivotal role in the transmission of the *Ṣaḥīḥ*.[2] Countless experts in the field of Ḥadīth have narrated ḥadīths via Firabrī directly (e.g. Ibn as-Sakan[3] and Ibn ʿAdī[4]) and indirectly (e.g. Khaṭṭābī[5] and Bayhaqī[6]). After spending a relatively lengthy life in disseminating knowledge, Firabrī breathed his last in Shawwāl 320 AH. May Allah have mercy on his soul![7]

Scholars have explicitly and implicitly[8] vouched for his credibil-

---

1 Spuler, "Firabr" in *the Encyclopedia of Islam*, Second Edition. Historians debated the vowelization of Firabr. Some pronounced it as Farabr while others maintained that it was Firabr. See Ibn Rushayd, *Ifādat an-Naṣīḥ*, 11–14.

2 As mentioned previously, Dhahabī does not accept Firabrī's statement, "90,000 people heard the *Ṣaḥīḥ* of Muḥammad ibn Ismāʿīl, and no one besides me remains who transmits it from him."

3 Dhahabī, *Tārīkh al-Islām*, 7:375.

4 See, for instance, Ibn ʿAdī, *Kāmil*, 1:123. In fact, Ibn ʿAdī was an important transmitter of the *Ṣaḥīḥ* via Firabrī in Jurjān. See Brown, *The Canonization of al-Bukhārī and Muslim*, 129.

5 Khaṭṭābī, *Aʿlām al-Ḥadīth*, 1:106.

6 See, for instance, Bayhaqī, *as-Sunan al-Kubrā*, 5:93, no. 9110; idem, *Shuʿab al-Īmān*, 4:421, no. 2750.

7 Dhahabī, *Siyar Aʿlām an-Nubalāʾ*, 15:10–13.

8 On the concept of implicit accreditation (*tawthīq ḍimnī*), see ʿAwwāmah, *Dirāsāt al-Kāshif*, 39–43.

ity. Abū 'l-Walīd al-Bājī (d. 474 AH) states that Firabrī was "reliable, prominent"[1] and Abū Bakr as-Samʿānī (d. 520 AH) adds that he was "scrupulous."[2] In his biographical dictionary of impugned transmitters, Ibn ʿAdī (d. 365 AH) set out to include every transmitter who was weak in his opinion and exclude those he believed were reliable.[3] Despite narrating from Firabrī multiple times in his book, Ibn ʿAdī does not include an entry on him nor does he negatively comment about him.[4] That a host of students and scholars alike have flocked from distant lands to transmit the *Ṣaḥīḥ* from Firabrī speaks volumes about his status as a transmitter. It is no wonder that he was, as Rushāṭī (d. 547 AH) explains, the main reference in transmitting the *Ṣaḥīḥ*.[5]

There are multiple recensions of *Ṣaḥīḥ al-Bukhārī* besides Firabrī's, including that of Ibrāhīm ibn Maʿqil (d. 295 AH) and Ḥammād ibn Shākir (d. 311 AH).[6] Firabrī's rise to prominence—vis-à-vis the *Ṣaḥīḥ* in comparison to his fellow transmitters—can be credited, in part, to his frequent studies under Bukhārī, access to the original manuscript, his recension being the most complete and a long lifespan.[7]

Given the preponderance of evidence to suggest his credibility, to argue that he was unreliable would require cogent proof to the contrary. For argument's sake, even if there was nothing explicit or implicit to vouch for his reliability, the default position of someone

1 Bājī, *at-Taʿdīl wa 't-Tajrīḥ*, 1:173.

2 Ibn Nuqṭah, *Taqyīd*, 126.

3 Ibn ʿAdī, *Kāmil*, 1:78–79, 241 and 302.

4 See, for instance, ibid., 1:123, 1:359 and 5:408.

5 Ibn Rushayd, *Ifādat an-Naṣīḥ*, 15 and 16.

6 The claim that Ibrāhīm ibn Maʿqil's recension lacks 300 hadīths that are found in Firabrī's recension is an exaggeration. Dr Shifā' al-Faqīh estimates that the number is 64 ḥadīths. See Shifā', *Riwāyāt al-Jāmiʿ aṣ-Ṣaḥīḥ li 'l-Imām al-Bukhārī*, 62–65; Sallūm, "Introduction," in ʿAdad Jamīʿ Ḥadīth al-Jamiʿ aṣ-Ṣaḥīḥ, 16–17; Sāmiḥ Mutawallī, *Ziyādāt al-Imām Muḥammad ibn Yūsuf ibn Maṭar al-Firabrī ʿalā Ṣaḥīḥ al-Bukhārī*, 26. The variation of 64 ḥadīths in a text that contains, as mentioned earlier, a total of 10,687 reports (i.e. rougly 0.6% of the Ṣaḥīḥ) is insignificant. Furthermore, the disparity in the number of ḥadīths each recension contains stems from the amount each transmitter was able to study under Bukhārī. It does not stem from a disagreement on the actual number of ḥadīths in the *Ṣaḥīḥ*. See Ibn Ḥajar, *Nukat*, 1:294; cf. Brown, *The Canonization of al-Bukhārī and Muslim*, 385.

7 Mutawallī, *Ziyādāt*, 24–29.

characterized with knowledge is that of uprightness, as explained by the Mālikī Ḥadīth expert Ibn ʿAbd al-Barr (d. 463 AH).[1] Concluding his biographical entry on Firabrī, Ibn Rushayd states that those who ask about his credibility should receive Yaḥyā ibn Maʿīn's reply to a person who asked about the credibility of some leading Ḥadīth scholars: "Hey lunatic, have you seen anyone ask about the likes of these people?"[2]

1 Ibn ʿAbd al-Barr, *Muqaddimat at-Tamhīd*, in *Khams Rasāʾil fī ʿUlūm al-Ḥadīth*, 88–92; ʿAwwāmah, annotations on *Tadrīb ar-Rāwī*, 4:19–21. It should be emphasized that the maxim applied here is for argument's sake, because its accurate application is in the case of unknown transmitters. In our case, there is sufficient proof to verify Firabrī's standing among transmitters. Shaykh ʿAbd al-Fattāḥ explains that the academic heritage left by scholars is evidence of their rank. The dearth of explicit approval or detailed biographies has no bearing on their reliability. He adds a couplet of poetry, which ends with, "The Night of Power (*Laylat al-Qadar*) is hidden, yet it is the best of nights." See Abū Ghuddah, *Khams Rasāʾil*, 92.

2 Ibn Rushayd, *Ifādat an-Naṣīḥ*, 15–16.

Translator's Appendix 2

ṢAGHĀNĪ'S MANUSCRIPT OF ṢAḤĪḤ AL-BUKHĀRĪ

Modern concerns surrounding the disappearance of *Ṣaḥīḥ al-Bukhārī*'s exemplar stem from a failure to grasp the nuances of Ḥadīth transmission. Consequently, Alphonse Mingana (d. 1937 CE), for one, has erroneously criticized the authorship of *Ṣaḥīḥ al-Bukhārī*.[1] In general, Ḥadīth scholars deemed oral transmission as the most authoritative method of establishing ḥadīths and were, therefore, not as concerned with the disappearance of original manuscripts.[2] The transmission of *Ṣaḥīḥ al-Bukhārī*, Qasṭallānī (d. 932 AH) explains, rests primarily on the medium of oral transmission, not on manuscripts.[3]

However, these concerns can be relatively assuaged by the presence of a valuable manuscript that was cross-referenced with Firabrī's (d. 320 AH) holograph: Raḍī ad-Dīn aṣ-Ṣaghānī's (d. 650 AH) manuscript of *Ṣaḥīḥ al-Bukhārī*. Given Firabrī's acquaintance with Bukhārī, frequent study of the *Ṣaḥīḥ* under him,[4] and access to Bukhārī's exemplar, his manuscript of the *Ṣaḥīḥ* was on par with the original. As such, the significance of a manuscript that was cross-referenced

1 Mingana, "An Important Ms. of Bukhārī's *Ṣaḥīḥ*," in *The Journal of the Royal Asiatic Society of Great Britain and Ireland* 2 (1936), 289.

2 ʿAbd al-Qādir Jalāl, *Iʿlāʾ al-Bukhārī*, 63.

3 Qasṭallānī, *Irshād as-Sārī*, 1:24.

4 As stated earlier, Firabrī studied the *Ṣaḥīḥ* under Bukhārī for the first time in Firabr in 248 AH, the second time in Bukhara in 252 AH, and the third time again in Firabr in 253, 254 and 255 AH. See Ibn Nuqṭah, *Taqyīd*, 126; Mutawallī, *Ziyādāt*, 29–31; Ṣāliḥ Fatḥī, "Nuskhat Ṣaḥīḥ al-Bukhārī," 80–84.

with Firabrī's holograph cannot be overstressed. This appendix will shed light on Ṣaghānī's biography and the value of his manuscript of the *Ṣaḥīḥ*.

Biography

The Ḥanafī lexicographer Raḍī ad-Dīn al-Ḥasan was born in Lahore 577 AH. He owes his sobriquet "Ṣaghānī" to his ancestral land in the upper Oxus province of Chāghāniyān—Arabicized to Ṣāghāniyān.[1] After receiving his primary education in Ghaznah (present-day Afghanistan), his academic travels took him to the broader Indian subcontinent, Yemen, Makkah and Baghdad (at the Niẓāmiyyah). In 617 AH, while in Baghdad, he served as an envoy to India for the Abbasid caliph Nāṣir and later for Mustanṣir.[2] He was a polymath and a prolific author,[3] described by Dimyāṭī (d. 705 AH) as an "authority in language, Islamic law and Ḥadīth."[4]

His forte was lexicography; he wrote a 20-volume compendium entitled *al-ʿUbāb az-Zākhir*. He wielded an equally strong command of the disciplines of Ḥadīth, as evidenced by his countless works like *Mashāriq al-Anwār* (a digest of the *Ṣaḥīḥayn* celebrated as the earliest contribution to Ḥadīth from an Indian scholar[5]), a gloss on *Ṣaḥīḥ al-Bukhārī*, a biographical dictionary on Bukhārī's teachers,[6] and treatises on forgeries,[7] to name the most prominent.[8] In addition, he

1 Raḥmān ʿAlī, *Tadhkirah Ulamā-e Hind* (trans. Zayn al-ʿĀbidīn al-Aʿẓamī), 86; Ramzi Baalbaki, "aṣ-Ṣaghānī," in *Encyclopedia of Islam*, Second Edition; Ibn as-Sāʿī, *ad-Durr ath-Thamīn*, 344. Ṣaghān is also known as Ṣāghān with an elongated *alif*. See Ḥamawī, *Muʿjam al-Udabāʾ*, 3:1015; Hijrānī, *Qilādat an-Naḥr*, 5:311.

2 Ibn as-Sāʿī, *ad-Durr ath-Thamīn*, 344; Ibn al-Fuwaṭī, *Majmaʿ al-Ādāb*, 6:490.

3 He is also recognized for his unique style of writing. For instance, beneath the letter *sīn*, he would write a letter *sīn* in a lower font to avoid confusing it for the letter *shīn*. On Ṣaghānī's style of writing, see Khān, "Introduction," in *Murtajal*, 11; Abū Ghuddah, footnotes on *Taṣḥīḥ al-Kutub*, 28.

4 Dhahabī, *Tārīkh al-Islām*, 14:637.

5 Ramzi Baalbaki, "Ṣaghānī," in *Encyclopedia of Islam*, Second Edition.

6 Sezgin, *Tārīkh at-Turāth al-ʿArabī*, 1:252.

7 For historical context on these treatises, see Karagözoglu, *Contested Avenues in Post-Classical Sunnī Ḥadīth Criticism*, 167–68.

8 Dhahabī, *Tārīkh al-Islām*, 14:636–638. On his expertise in Ḥadīth, see Chishtī,

mastered Khaṭṭābī's *Maʿālim as-Sunan* and counseled his students to memorize al-Qāsim ibn Sallām's *Gharīb al-Ḥadīth*.[1] He passed away on 19 Shaʿbān 650 AH, in Baghdad, but his body was relocated to Makkah where he was buried according to his final wishes.[2]

Ṣaghānī's Manuscript of the Ṣaḥīḥ

As his oeuvre suggests, Ṣaghānī took special interest in Bukhārī's *Ṣaḥīḥ*. Furthermore, he studied the *Ṣaḥīḥ* under several direct students of Abū 'l-Waqt as-Sijzī (d. 553 AH), a key transmitter of the work.[3] During his stay in Baghdad, Ṣaghānī spent a considerable amount of time editing a particular manuscript of *Ṣaḥīḥ al-Bukhārī*, later entitled the Baghdādī manuscript. This was not the first manuscript of the *Ṣaḥīḥ* that he wrote. Earlier while sojourning in Aden, Yemen, he transcribed several manuscripts, which he left there as endowments.[4] The most notable value of the Baghdādī manuscript lies in Ṣaghānī's cross-analysis of it with another key manuscript: Firabrī's holograph.[5]

The reader may recall that Firabrī had access to Bukhārī's exemplar that was transcribed by his copyist Abū Jaʿfar al-Warrāq.[6] A close reading of Ṣaghānī's manuscript further reveals that he had access to Ibrāhīm ibn Maʿqil's (d. 295 AH) recension, a direct transmitter from Bukhārī.[7] In many places, Ṣaghānī alludes to material found exclusively in Firabrī's manuscript, e.g. commentary and preferences

---

Imām-e Lughat Ḥasan ibn Muḥammad aṣ-Ṣāghānī al-Lāhorī 2, 131–136. In the 1959 edition of the monthly *Maʿārif* magazine, Maulana ʿAbd al-Ḥalīm Chishtī contributed nine columns (January to September) on the life and times of Ṣaghānī.

1 Ḥamawī, *Muʿjam al-Udabāʾ*, 3:1015.

2 Ibn al-Fuwaṭī, *Majmaʿ al-Ādāb*, 6:490.

3 Dhahabī, *Tārīkh al-Islām*, 14:637; idem, *Siyar Aʿlām an-Nubalāʾ*, 22:97; Yūsufān, *al-Muḥaddith aṣ-Ṣaghānī wa Nuskhatuhu min aṣ-Ṣaḥīḥ*, 3.

4 Abū Makhramah, *Tārīkh Thaghr ʿAdan*, 86.

5 Ibn Ḥajar, *Fatḥ al-Bārī*, 1:153.

6 Aʿẓamī, "Introduction," in *al-Jāmiʿ al-Musnad aṣ-Ṣaḥīḥ*, 15; Sezgin, *Tārīkh at-Turāth al-ʿArabī*, 1:226; cf. Shifāʾ, *Riwāyāt al-Jāmiʿ aṣ-Ṣaḥīḥ*, 429–30. That Firabrī gained access to Bukhārī's exemplar through Abū Jaʿfar al-Warrāq explains how the manuscript came to be in his possession after Bukhārī's demise.

7 Mutawallī, *Ziyādāt*, 12.

from Bukhārī,[1] added information on the transmitters[2] and continuity of truncated chains.[3] In one place, he consults Firabrī's manuscript to respond to Ismāʿīlī's critique of Bukhārī.[4] Dr Sāmiḥ Mutawallī details the locations of at least ten copies of Ṣaghānī's manuscript in libraries throughout Turkey, Saudi Arabia and England.[5]

Further underscoring the value of this manuscript, subsequent scholars have put it to good use. Distinguished commentators on the *Ṣaḥīḥ* like Shams ad-Dīn al-Kirmānī (d. 786 AH),[6] Badr ad-Dīn al-ʿAynī (d. 855 AH),[7] Ibn Ḥajar al-ʿAsqalānī (d. 852 AH)[8] and Shihāb ad-Dīn al-Qasṭallānī (d. 923 AH)[9] have cited material from Ṣaghānī's

1 For instance, under ḥadīth no. 1511, the words "Abū ʿAbdillāh said: He intends Banū Nāfiʿ" are added.

2 For instance, under ḥadīth no. 6433, the words "He is Ḥumrān ibn Abān" are added.

3 For instance, ḥadīth no. 229 is transmitted via ʿAbdullāh ibn Ṣāliḥ from al-Layth. In any case, under no. 2063, the ḥadīth is repeated with a continuous chain in the other manuscripts. See Yūsufān, *al-Muḥaddith aṣ-Ṣaghānī*, 7–10; Sallūm, *Nuskhat al-Imām aṣ-Ṣaghānī min Ṣaḥīḥ al-Bukhārī wa Qīmatuhā al-ʿIlmiyyah* in alukah.net/library/0/39186 (last accessed 10/15/2018).

4 ʿUtaybī, *Kitāb Jabr*, 285–86. There is only one instance where Ṣaghānī's manuscript contains an additional Prophetic ḥadīth. Under ḥadīth no. 63, Bukhārī transmits the famous exchange between Ḍimām ibn Thaʿlabah and the Prophet ﷺ. In all other manuscripts, he then follows it with an alternative chain of transmission and alludes to the previous ḥadīth. By contrast, Ṣaghānī's manuscript repeats the entire text with the alternative chain, not only an allusion to it. See Ibn Ḥajar, *Fatḥ al-Bārī*, 1:150; Sallūm, "Introduction," in *ʿAdad Jamīʿ Ḥadīth al-Jamiʿ aṣ-Ṣaḥīḥ*, 7. It also contains one extra non-Prophetic report from Ibn ʿAbbās on the expiation of the one unable to fast due to old age. See Nadwī, *Nuskhat al-Imām aṣ-Ṣaghānī*, 270.

5 Mutawallī, *Ziyādāt*, 16–17; ʿUtaybī, *Kitāb Jabr*, 281–86. Dr Taqī ad-Dīn an-Nadwī writes about a manuscript located in Pakistan. See Nadwī, *Nuskhat al-Imām aṣ-Ṣaghānī li-Ṣaḥīḥ al-Imām al-Bukhārī: Dirāsah wa Taḥlīl*, 267.

6 Kirmānī, *al-Kawākib ad-Darārī*, 19:241.

7 ʿAynī, *ʿUmdat al-Qārī*, 25:102.

8 While highlighting the value of Ṣaghānī's manuscript, Maulana Anwār Shāh al-Kashmīrī (d. 1933) writes that although Ḥāfiẓ Ibn Ḥajar had access to the manuscript, he may have not utilized it to its full potential. See Kashmīrī, *Fayḍ al-Bārī*, 1:33; cf. Abshar ʿAwaḍ, *Juhūd al-Imāmayn al-Ḥāfiẓ al-Yūnīnī wa 'l-Ḥāfīz Ibn Ḥajar*, 29–30. After comparing the manuscript with *Fatḥ al-Bārī*, Nadwī notes several instances where Ibn Ḥajar did not allude to material found in the manuscript. See Nadwī, *Nuskhat al-Imām aṣ-Ṣaghānī*, 270–78, nos. 2, 5, 8, 9 and 10.

9 Qasṭallānī, *Irshād as-Sārī*, 1:205.

manuscript. In his magnum opus, *Fatḥ al-Bārī*, Ibn Ḥajar cites the manuscript over 100 times.[1]

The Indian lithographic print of the *Ṣaḥīḥ*, meticulously produced with marginal notes by Aḥmad ʿAlī as-Sahāranpūrī (d. 1297 AH/1880 CE), is an invaluable yet underappreciated work of scholarship.[2] Sahāranpūrī spent ten years critically analyzing and refining his personal copy of the *Ṣaḥīḥ* with a number of important manuscripts like that of his teacher Shāh Muḥammad Isḥāq (d. 1262 AH), an extension of ʿAbdullāh ibn Sālim al-Baṣrī's legendary copy.[3] Between 1851–1854 CE—decades before the celebrated Amīriyyah edition[4]—he produced the earliest print of the *Ṣaḥīḥ* in two volumes through his Delhi-based printing house, Maṭbaʿ Aḥmadī.[5] Most important for our purposes, he had at his disposal Ṣaghānī's manuscript, for which he used the symbols *ṣād/ghayn*.[6] There are instances where Sahāranpūrī noted variants from Ṣaghānī that his fellow commentators did not draw attention to—not even Ibn Ḥajar.[7]

---

1 Nadwī, *Nuskhat al-Imām aṣ-Ṣaghānī*, 257.

2 Sahāranpūrī's critical work has recently been printed by Dār al-Bashā'ir al-Islāmiyyah with editorial work by Dr Taqī ad-Dīn an-Nadwī.

3 Ḥasanī, *Nuzhat al-Khawāṭir*, 7:907; Nadwī, *Nuskhat al-Imām aṣ-Ṣaghānī*, 257; idem, "Introduction," in *al-Jāmiʿ al-Musnad aṣ-Ṣaḥīḥ*, 1:17–18.

4 The Amīriyyah edition was published in 1895. Sahāranpūrī's edition even predates the Brill (Leiden) edition that was published in 1862. Dr Aḥmad as-Sallūm opines that Sahāranpūrī's edition is superior to the Amīriyyah edition because it cites manuscript-variants more frequently. See Sallūm, "Introduction," in *al-Mukhtaṣar an-Naṣīḥ*, 1:92.

5 Nūr al-Ḥasan Kandhlawī, *Ustādh al-Kull*, 412–13; Muḥammad Rustum, *al-Jāmiʿ aṣ-Ṣaḥīḥ li 'l-Imām al-Bukhārī wa ʿInāyat al-Ummah al-Islāmiyyah bihi Sharqan wa Gharban*, 43. Under the auspices of Sahāranpūrī, Maṭbaʿ Aḥmadī critically edited and published a number of important Ḥadīth books which hitherto have never been printed, such as *Ṣaḥīḥ Muslim*, *Jāmiʿ at-Tirmidhī* and *Mishkāt al-Maṣābīḥ*. See Kandhlawī, *Ustādh al-Kull*, 409 and 413.

6 In the introduction to his edition, Sahāranpūrī lists the symbols he used throughout the work. See Sahāranpūrī, "Introduction," in *al-Jāmiʿ al-Musnad aṣ-Ṣaḥīḥ*, 104–7. For a detailed study of Sahāranpūrī's work on *Ṣaḥīḥ al-Bukhārī*, see my paper "*Ḥadīth Scholarship in the Indian Subcontinent: Mawlānā Aḥmad ʿAlī al-Sahāranpūrī and the First Print of Ṣaḥīḥ al-Bukhārī*."

7 See, for instance, Nadwī, *Nuskhat al-Imām aṣ-Ṣaghānī*, 270–74, nos. 2, 8 and 9; idem, "Introduction," in *al-Jāmiʿ al-Musnad aṣ-Ṣaḥīḥ*, 1:19–23.

Conclusion

As contentions surrounding the disappearance of Bukhārī's exemplar continue to arise, one should bear in mind the famous maxim: unawareness of something is not proof of its nonexistence. Countless manuscripts that were once assumed to have vanished have recently been rediscovered.[1] However, even if Bukhārī's exemplar does not resurface, it will not affect the veracity of the text. The practice of oral tradition has preserved this text from adulteration,[2] not to mention the presence of critically-acclaimed secondary and tertiary copies. Having been cross-referenced with Firabrī's holograph—a manuscript that is on par with the exempar—Ṣaghānī's manuscript of the *Ṣaḥīḥ* has preserved for us an accessible, near replica of the original.

1 For a study of early Islamic papyri that have been recently discovered, see Nabia Abbott's *Studies in Arabic Literary Papyri I: Historical Texts* and *Studies in Arabic Literary Papyri II: Qur'ānic Commentary and Tradition*.

2 This is not to negate the presence of variations between the manuscripts of the *Ṣaḥīḥ*. The variations between the recensions of the *Ṣaḥīḥ* fall under one of the following categories: (i) general variations (e.g. arrangement and titles of chapters); (ii) *isnād*-based (e.g. phrases of transmission); and (iii) text-based (e.g. addition of a word or letter). But these variations are not serious. They do not affect the rank of the *Ṣaḥīḥ* or cast doubt on the authenticity of its ḥadīths. As any specialist will tell you, it is absolutely normal for such variations to occur. See ʿAbd al-Qādir Jalāl, *Iʿlā' al-Bukhārī*, 65–71.

Translator's Appendix 3

The following are two pictures of Nuwayrī's 5th handwritten copy of the Yūnīniyyah.

The first page

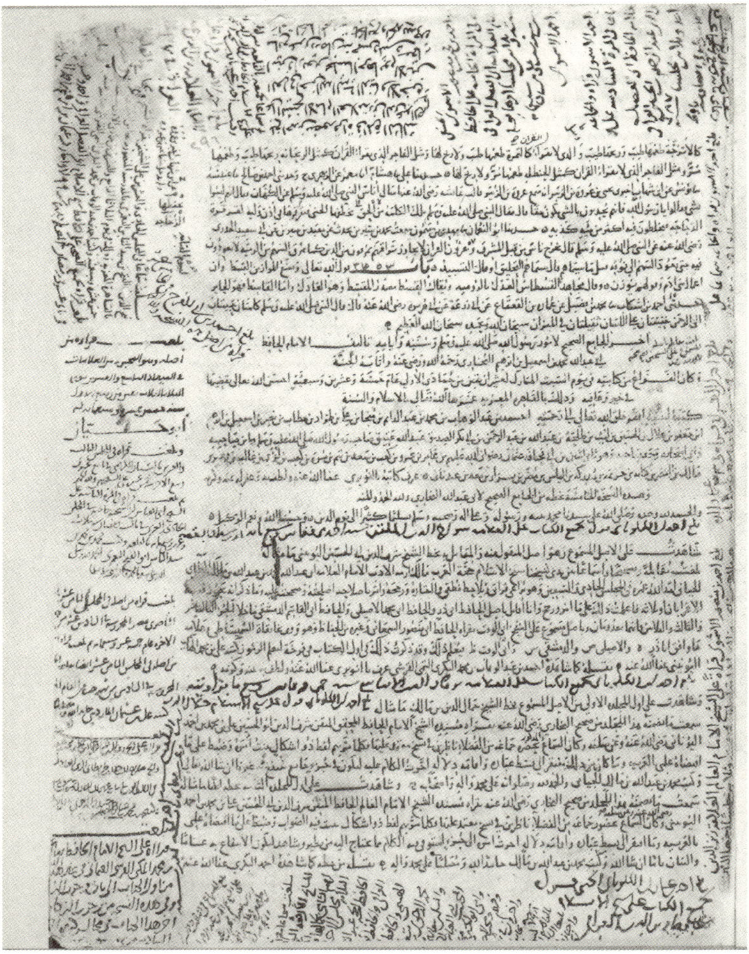

Final page and reading certificates

Selected Bibliography

ʿAbd al-Ḥalīm, Jumuʿah Fatḥī. *Riwāyāt al-Jāmiʿ aṣ-Ṣaḥīḥ wa Nusakhuhu: Dirāsah Naẓariyyah Taṭbīqiyyah*. Doha: Wizārat al-Awqāf wa ash-Shu'ūn al-Islāmiyyah, 2013.

Abū Dāwūd, Sulaymān ibn al-Ashʿath. *Sunan*. Ed. Shuʿayb al-Arna'ūt. 7 vols. Beirut: ar-Risālah al-ʿĀlamiyyah, 2009.

Abū Ghuddah, ʿAbd al-Fattāḥ. *Ṣafḥah Mushriqah min Tārīkh Samāʿ al-Ḥadīth ʿind al-Muḥaddithīn*. Aleppo: Maktab al-Maṭbūʿāt al-Islāmiyyah, 1992.

———. *al-Isnād min ad-Dīn*. Aleppo: Maktab al-Maṭbūʿāt al-Islāmiyyah, 1992.

———. *Lamaḥāt min Tārīkh as-Sunnah wa ʿUlūm al-Ḥadīth*. Beirut: Dār al-Bashā'ir al-Islāmiyyah, 1429 AH.

———. *Taḥqīq Ismay aṣ-Ṣaḥīḥayn wa Ism Jāmiʿ at-Tirmidhī*. Aleppo: Maktabat al-Maṭbūʿāt al-Islamiyyah, 1993.

———. *Thalāth Rasā'il fī ʿIlm Muṣṭalaḥ al-Ḥadīth*. Beirut: Dār al-Bashā'ir al-Islāmiyyah, 2005.

Al-Andalusī, al-Muhallab ibn Abī Ṣufrah. *al-Mukhtaṣar an-Naṣīḥ fī Tahdhīb al-Kitāb al-Jāmiʿ aṣ-Ṣaḥīḥ*. Ed. Aḥmad ibn Fāris as-Sallūm. Riyadh: Dār Ahl as-Sunnah, 1429 AH.

Al-ʿAsqalānī, Aḥmad ibn ʿAlī ibn Ḥajar. *ad-Durar al-Kāminah fī Aʿyān al-Mi'ah ath-Thāminah*. Hyderabad: Majlis Dā'irat al-Maʿārif al-ʿUthmāniyyah, 1972.

———. *Fatḥ al-Bārī Sharḥ Ṣaḥīḥ al-Bukhārī*. Ed. Bin Bāz et al. 13 vols. Cairo: al-Maktabah as-Salafiyyah, 1379 AH.

———. *Lisān al-Mīzān*. Ed. ʿAbd al-Fattāḥ Abū Ghuddah. Beirut: Dār al-Bashā'ir al-Islāmiyyah, 2002.

———. *An-Nukat ʿalā Kitāb Ibn aṣ-Ṣalāḥ*. Ed. Rabīʿ al-Madkhalī. 2 vols. Madīnah: al-Jāmiʿah al-Islāmiyyah, 1984.

———. *Taghlīq at-Taʿlīq ʿalā Ṣaḥīḥ al-Bukhārī*. Beirut: al-Maktab al-Islāmī, 1405 AH.

Aʿẓamī, Muḥammad Muṣṭafā. *Studies in Early Hadīth Literature with a Critical Edition of Some Early Texts*. Indianapolis: American Trust Publications, 1978.

Al-Baghdādī, Aḥmad ibn ʿAlī al-Khaṭīb. *Muwaḍḍiḥ Awhām al-Jamʿ wa 't-Tafrīq*. Ed. ʿAbd ar-Raḥmān al-Muʿallimī. Beirut: Dār al-Fikr, 1985.

———. *Sharaf Aṣḥāb al-Ḥadīth*. Ed. Muḥammad Saʿīd. Ankara: Dār Iḥyā' as-Sunnah an-Nabawiyyah, n.d.

———. *Tārīkh Madīnat as-Salām wa Akhbār Muḥaddithīhā wa Dhikr Quṭṭānihā al-ʿUlamā' min Ghayr Ahlihā wa Wāridīhā*. Ed. Bashshār ʿAwwād. 17 vols. Beirut: Dār al-Gharb al-Islāmī, 2001.

Al-Bājī, Abū 'l-Walīd Sulaymān. *At-Taʿdīl wa 't-Tajrīḥ li-man Kharraj ʿanhū 'l-Bukhārī fī 'l-Jāmiʿ aṣ-Ṣaḥīḥ*. Morocco: Wizārat al-Awqāf, n.d.

Al-Bayhaqī, Aḥmad ibn al-Ḥusayn. *al-Madkhal ilā ʿIlm as-Sunan*. Ed. Muḥammad ʿAwwāmah. Jeddah: Dār al-Minhāj, 2016.

———. *as-Sunan al-Kubrā*. Beirut: Dār al-Kutub al-ʿIlmiyyah, 2003.

Brown, Jonathan A.C. *Hadīth: Muhammad's Legacy in the Medival and Modern World*. Oxford: Oneworld Publications, 2009.

———. *The Canonization of al-Bukhārī and Muslim: The Formation and Function of the Sunnī Ḥadīth Canon*. Leiden: Brill, 2007.

———. *Misquoting Muhammad: The Challenge and Choices of Interpreting the Prophet's Legacy*. Oxford: Oneworld, 2014.

Al-Bukhārī, Muḥammad ibn Ismāʿīl. *al-Jāmiʿ al-Musnad aṣ-Ṣaḥīḥ*. Ed. Zuhayr Nāṣir. 9 vols. Beirut: Dār Ṭawq an-Najāh, 1422 AH.

———. *at-Tārīkh al-Kabīr*. Hyderabad: Dā'irat al-Maʿārif al-ʿUthmāniyyah, n.d.

Adh-Dhahabī, Muḥammad ibn Aḥmad. *Mīzān al-Iʿtidāl fī Naqd ar-Rijāl*. Ed. ʿAlī Muḥammad. 4 vols. Beirut: Dār al-Maʿrifah, 1963.

———. *Siyar Aʿlām an-Nubalā'*. Ed. Shuʿayb al-Arna'ūt et al. 25 vols. Beirut: Mu'assasat ar-Risālah, 1405 AH.

———. *Tadhkirat al-Ḥuffāẓ*. Ed. ʿAbd al-Raḥmān al-Muʿallimī. Vol. 4. Beirut: Dār al-Kutub al-ʿIllmiyyah, 1998.

———. *Tārīkh al-Islām*. Ed. Bashshār ʿAwwād Maʿrūf. Beirut: Dār al-Gharb al-Islāmī, 2003.

Ad-Dimashqī, Muḥammad ibn Nāṣir al-Dīn. *Tawḍīḥ al-Mushtabih fī Ḍabṭ Asmā' ar-Ruwāh wa Ansābihim wa Alqābihim wa Kunāhum*. Beirut: Mu'assasat ar-Risālah, 1993.

Ḥājjī Khalīfah, Muṣṭafā ibn ʿAbdillāh. *Kashf aẓ-Ẓunūn ʿan Asāmī al-Kutub wa 'l-Funūn*. Baghdad: Maktabat al-Muthannā, 1941.

Halal, Ṣāliḥ Fatḥī. "Nuskhat Ṣaḥīḥ al-Bukhārī al-Aṣliyyah wa Ashhar Riwāyātihi." *Majallat at-Turāth an-Nabawī* 3 (2018): 73–124.

Al-Ḥamawī, Yāqūt ibn ʿAbdillāh. *Muʿjam al-Udabā'*. Beirut: Dār al-Gharb al-Islāmī, 1993.

Al-Ḥasanī, ʿAbd al-Ḥayy ibn Fakhr ad-Dīn. *Nuzhat al-Khawāṭir wa Bahjat al-Masāmiʿ wa 'n-Nawāẓir*. Beirut: Ibn Ḥazm, 1999.

Al-Ḥasanī, Muḥammad Mujīr al-Khaṭīb. *Maʿrifat Madār al-Isnād wa Bayān Makānatihi fī ʿIlm ʿIlal al-Ḥadīth*. Riyadh: Dār al-Maymān, 2007.

Al-Haytamī, Aḥmad ibn Muḥammad ibn Ḥajar. *Fatḥ al-Ilāh fī Sharḥ al-Mishkāh*. Beirut: Dār al-Kutub al-ʿIlmiyyah, 2015.

Al-Ḥusaynī, Muḥammad ʿIṣām. *Itḥāf al-Qārī bi-Maʿrifat Juhūd wa Aʿmāl al-ʿUlamā' ʿalā Ṣaḥīḥ al-Bukhārī,*. Beirut: Dār al-Yamāmah, 1987.

Ibn ʿAsākir, Abū 'l-Qāsim ʿAlī. *Tārīkh Madīnat Dimashq*. Ed. ʿAmr al-ʿAmrawī. Beirut: Dār al-Fikr, 1995.

Ibn Ḥanbal, Abū ʿAbdillāh Aḥmad. *al-Musnad*. Ed. Shuʿayb al-Arna'ūt et al. Beirut: Mu'assasat al-Risālah, 1421 AH.

Ibn Ḥazm, ʿAlī ibn Aḥmad. *al-Fiṣal fī 'l-Milal wa 'n-Niḥal*. Cairo: Khānijī, n.d.

Ibn al-Jazarī, Muḥammad ibn Ibrāhīm. *Tārīkh Ḥawādīth az-Zamān wa Anbā'ihi wa Wafayāt al-Akābir wa 'l-Aʿyān min Abnā'ihi*. Beirut: al-Maktabah al-ʿAṣriyyah, 1998

Ibn Makūlā, ʿAlī ibn Hibatillāh. *al-Ikmāl fī Rafʿ al-Irtiyāb ʿan 'l-Mu'talif wa al-Mukhtalif fī 'l-Asmā' wa 'l-Kunā wa 'l-Ansāb*. Beirut: Dār al-Kutub al-ʿIlmiyyah, 1990.

Ibn Nuqṭah, Abū Bakr Muḥammad. *Ikmāl al-Ikmāl*. Makkah: Jāmiʿat Umm al-Qurā, 1410 AH.

———. *Al-Taqyīd li-Maʿrifat Ruwāt al-Sunan wa ʾl-Masānīd*. Ed. Abū Idrīs Sharīf. 2 vols. Beirut: Dār al-Nawādir, 2014.

Ibn Rajab, ʿAbd ar-Raḥmān ibn Aḥmad. *Dhayl Ṭabaqāt al-Ḥanābilah*. Riyadh: Maktabat al-ʿUbaykān, 2005.

Ibn Rushayd, Muḥammad ibn ʿUmar. *Ifādat an-Naṣīḥ fī ʾt-Taʿrīf bi-Sanad al-Jāmiʿ aṣ-Ṣaḥīḥ*. Tunis: ad-Dār at-Tūnasiyyah, n.d.

Ibn aṣ-Ṣalāḥ, ʿUthmān ibn ʿAbd ar-Raḥmān. *Maʿrifat Anwāʿ ʿIlm al-Ḥadīth*. Ed. Nūr ad-Dīn ʿItr. Beirut: Dār al-Fikr, 2009.

Al-Idlibī, Ṣalāḥ ad-Dīn ibn Aḥmad. *Manhaj Naqd al-Matn ʿind ʿUlamāʾ al-Ḥadīth an-Nabawī*. Beirut: Dār al-Āfāq al-Jadīdah, 1983.

Al-Ishbīlī, Ibn Khayr. *Fihrist*. Ed. Bashshār ʿAwwād Maʿrūf. Beirut: Dār al-Gharb al-Islāmī, 2009.

ʿIyāḍ ibn Mūsā al-Qāḍī. *Al-Ilmāʿ ilā Maʿrifat Uṣūl al-Riwāyah wa Taqyīd as-Samāʿ*. Cairo: Maktabat Dār at-Turāth, 1970.

Jalāl, ʿAbd al-Qādir ibn Muḥammad. *Iʿlāʾ al-Bukhārī: Tathbīt Makānat al-Imām al-Bukhārī wa Ṣaḥīḥihi min Khilāl Radd ash-Shubuhāt Ḥawlahumā*. Riyadh: Dār Salaf, 2018.

Al-Kattānī, Muḥammad ʿAbd al-Ḥayy. *Fahras al-Fahāris*. Beirut: Dār al-Gharb al-Islāmī, 1982.

Al-Kattānī, Muḥammad ibn Jaʿfar. *Ar-Risālah al-Mustaṭrafah li-Bayān Mashhūr Kutub as-Sunnah al-Musharrafah*. Beirut: Dār al-Bashāʾir al-Islāmiyyah, 2007.

Al-Khalīlī, Abū Yaʿlā Khalīl. *al-Irshād fī Maʿrifat ʿUlamāʾ al-Ḥadīth*. Riyadh: Maktabat ar-Rushd, 1409 AH.

Al-Khaṭṭābī, Ḥamd ibn Muḥammad. *Aʿlām al-Ḥadīth*. Makkah: Jāmiʿat Umm al-Qurā, 1988.

Al-Maqrīzī, Aḥmad ibn ʿAlī. *al-Mawāʿiẓ wa ʾl-Iʿtibār bi-Dhikr al-Khiṭaṭ wa ʾl-Āthār*. Beirut: Dār al-Kutub al-ʿIlmiyyah, 1997.

Al-Maʿṣarānī, Muḥammad Aḥmad. "Tajalliyāt al-Jamāl fī Nuskhat al-Jāmiʿ aṣ-Ṣaḥīḥ li ʾl-Bukhārī bi-Khaṭṭ al-Nuwayrī Dirāsah wa Taḥqīq." *Majallat at-Turāth an-Nabawī* 3 (2018): 11–72.

Al-Mizzī, Jamāl ad-Dīn Yūsuf. *Tuḥfat al-Ashrāf bi-Maʿrifat al-Aṭrāf*. Ed. Bashshār ʿAwwād Maʿrūf. Beirut: Dār al-Gharb al-Islāmī, 1999.

Al-Mubārakfūrī, ʿAbd as-Salām. *Sīrat al-Imām al-Bukhārī*. Ed. ʿAbd al-ʿAlīm al-Bastawī. Makkah: Dār ʿĀlam al-Fawā'id, 2001.

Al-Mundhirī, ʿAbd al-ʿAẓīm. *Jawāb al-Ḥāfiẓ Abī Muḥammad ʿAbd al-ʿAẓīm al-Mundhirī al-Miṣrī ʿan As'ilah fī 'l-Jarḥ wa 't-Taʿdīl*. Ed. ʿAbd al-Fattāḥ Abū Ghuddah. Aleppo: Maktab al-Maṭbūʿāt al-Islāmiyyah, 1411 AH.

Mutawallī, Sāmiḥ ʿAbdullāh. *Ziyādāt al-Imām Muḥammad ibn Yūsuf ibn Maṭar al-Firabrī ʿalā Ṣaḥīḥ al-Bukhārī*. Jeddah: Dār al-Awrāq ath-Thaqāfiyyah, 2017.

An-Nasafī, Najm ad-Dīn ʿUmar. *al-Qand fī ʿUlamā' Samarqand*. Riyadh: Maktabat al-Kawthar, 1991.

An-Nawawī, Yaḥyā ibn Sharaf. *at-Talkhīṣ Sharḥ al-Jāmiʿ aṣ-Ṣaḥīḥ*. Riyadh: Dār Ṭayyibah, 2008.

An-Naysābūrī, al-Ḥākim Muḥammad ibn ʿAbdillāh. *al-Madkhal ilā Maʿrifat Kitāb al-Iklīl*. Ed. Aḥmad Fāris. Beirut: Dār Ibn Ḥazm, 2003.

———. *al-Mustadrak ʿalā aṣ-Ṣaḥīḥayn*. Ed. Muṣṭafā ʿAṭā. Beirut: Dār al-Kutub al-ʿIlmiyyah, 1990.

An-Nuwayrī, Aḥmad ibn ʿAbd al-Wahhāb. *Nihāyat al-Arab fī Funūn al-Adab*. Cairo: Dār al-Kutub wa 'l-Wathā'iq al-Qawmiyyah, 1423 AH.

Al-Qasṭallānī, Aḥmad ibn Muḥammad. *Irshād as-Sārī li-Sharḥ Ṣaḥīḥ al-Bukhārī*. Cairo: al-Maṭbaʿah al-Amīriyyah, 1323 AH.

As-Sahmī, Ḥamzah ibn Yūsuf. *Tārīkh Jurjān*. Beirut: ʿĀlam al-Kutub, 1987.

As-Sakhāwī, Muḥammad ibn ʿAbd ar-Raḥmān. *Fatḥ al-Mughīth bi-Sharḥ Alfiyyat al-Ḥadīth*. Ed. ʿAbd al-Karīm al-Khuḍayr and Muḥammad ibn ʿAbdillāh. Riyadh: Dār al-Minhāj, 2005.

As-Samʿānī, ʿAbd al-Karīm ibn Muḥammad. *Ansāb*. Hyderabad: Majlis Dā'irat al-Maʿārif, 1962.

Aṣ-Ṣarīfīnī, Ibrāhīm ibn Muḥammad. *al-Muntakhab min as-Siyāq li-Tārīkh Naysābūr*. Beirut: Dār al-Kutub al-ʿIlmiyyah, 1989.

Sezgin, Fuat. *Tārīkh al-Turāth al-ʿArabī*. Trans. Maḥmūd Ḥijāzī. Riyadh: Jāmiʿat al-Imām Muḥammad ibn Saʿūd, 1991.

As-Shāmī, Ṣāliḥ Aḥmad. *Maʿālim as-Sunnah an-Nabawiyyah*. Damascus: Dār al-Qalam, 2015.

As-Subkī, ʿAbd al-Wahhāb ibn Taqī ad-Dīn. *Ṭabaqāt ash-Shāfiʿiyyah al-Kubrā*.

Ed. al-Ḥilw and al-Ṭanāḥī. 10 vols. Cairo: Fayṣal al-Bābī al-Ḥalabī, 1413 AH.

As-Suyūṭī, ʿAbd ar-Raḥmān ibn Abī Bakr. *Tadrīb ar-Rāwī fī Sharḥ Taqrīb an-Nawāwī*. Ed. Muḥammad ʿAwwāmah. Jeddah: Dār al-Minhāj, 2016.

At-Tirhutī, Muḥammad Muḥsin ibn Yahyā. *al-Yāniʿ al-Janī min Asānīd ash-Shaykh ʿAbd al-Ghanī*. Amman: Arwiqah, 2016.

At-Tirmidhī, Muḥammad ibn ʿĪsā. *al-ʿIlal al-Kabīr*. Beirut: ʿĀlam al-Kutub, 1989.

Al-ʿUtaybī, Abū Hāshim Ḥāfiẓ. *Kitāb Jabr wa huwa at-Tārīkh al-Mukhtaṣar li'l-Jāmiʿ aṣ-Ṣaḥīḥ al-Musnad al-Mukhtaṣar*. Cairo: Dār at-Ta'ṣīl, 2018.